READINGS IN 1 KINGS

An Interpretation Arranged for Personal
and Group Bible Study

With Questions and Notes

*To
Stewart
Murray
and
Craig*

READINGS IN 1 KINGS

An Interpretation Arranged for Personal and Group Bible Study

With Questions and Notes

RONALD S. WALLACE

WILLIAM B. EERDMANS PUBLISHING COMPANY
GRAND RAPIDS, MICHIGAN

First published 1995 by
Scottish Academic Press Ltd.
56 Hanover Street, Edinburgh EH2 2DX Scotland

This edition published 1996
through special arrangement with Scottish Academic Press by
Wm. B. Eerdmans Publishing Co.
255 Jefferson Ave. S.E., Grand Rapids, Michigan 49503

Printed in the United States of America

00 99 98 97 96   7 6 5 4 3 2 1

Library of Congress Cataloging-in-Publication Data

Wallace, Ronald S.
Readings in 1 Kings: an interpretation arranged for personal and
group Bible study with questions and notes / by Ronald S. Wallace.
p.   cm.
ISBN 0-8028-4200-3 (pbk.: alk. paper)
1. Bible. O.T. Kings, 1st — Criticism, interpretation, etc.
I. Title.
BS1335.2W35   1995
222′.5307 — dc20   95-40216
CIP

CONTENTS

FOREWORD

I have always been encouraged by the appreciative reception given to the biblical expositions I have published, especially by lay readers and fellow pastors. An important development within more recent years in the Church has been the growing number of house groups for Bible study. On my recent visit to teach in Singapore I was made aware of the need for material which could be used for these. Christ is seeking to interpret Holy Scripture within the Church not only through the ministry of scholar and pastor but also through that of dedicated and informed laity, and a wise and sensitive pastor is one who has learned to seek the message of the Bible not only on behalf of his people but also along with them.

Though I have no longer the privilege of a congregation or class of my own I still find the Old Testament so meaningful and relevant to the situation as I see it in Church today, that I cannot refrain from seeking to make some contribution to the literature at the disposal of the student or preacher. In the light of Christ and the New Testament, and with the traditional background of the thought and exegesis of the Church in my mind, I have tried to express as clearly as I can the thoughts with which I find myself enlightened, challenged, comforted and encouraged by these stories and texts. I must admit that there are occasional echoes of sermons I preached years ago, and of more academic lectures I gave in class. But my main purpose has been to give fresh thoughts fresh clothing, and to write in the light of further experience, study and observation.

The narrative in the book of Kings, does not lend itself to be cut up into short and satisfying 'Daily Bible Readings'. To appreciate what it says, it has to be over-viewed, often in quite lengthy sections. With the limited devotional time at the disposal of the average church member, each of these would normally take several days to absorb and think over. Therefore the book is ideal for weekly study groups, and for personal study by a reader who is willing patiently to hold in the mind several stories which have been deliberately placed together by an editor so that the drift of the history can be most fully understood. I have to admit that occasionally the division has had to be artificially made to fit into the pattern of such regular study, and to avoid dwelling too long on passages that might not be of any vital interest, but I have tried to find for each section a unified message which I have considered under subtitles. Here and there I have added notes to give extra information where it might be needed, to help to clarify further aspects of the text or to explain and justify the approach I have made. For each section I have appended a series of points for further discussion mostly in the form of questions. It must be remembered that group discussion might be most profitable if it concentrated on the points brought out of the exposition, critically or otherwise. Instead of printing the whole lengthy text at the head of each section, I have indicated in a short introductory note the main historical facts to be noted by the reader as the whole passage is first read through.

Edinburgh, October 1994

ACKNOWLEDGEMENTS

I began writing this book as a contribution to the series of commentaries designed by Crossway Books for group Bible Study, and I am grateful to Rev Stephen Dray for encouraging me to begin. I discovered eventually, however, that the form in which I put things could not pass their editorial requirements, and I am grateful to Dr Douglas Grant for so trustingly accepting exactly what I write. I appreciate, too the help given by my daughter, Rev. Elizabeth Newlands, for taking over the supervision and typing of the manuscript, and by Rev. Dr R. B. W. Walker for correcting the proofs

I have to thank both the I. V. Press, and W. B. Eerdmans for the two illustrations on p. 51.

During the past sixty years when I preached, wrote and taught on the Book of Kings, I read everything available to me. I was always from the beginning indebted to Bishop Hall's *Contemplations,* and also, later, to Wilhelm Vischer's *Das Christus-Zeugnis des Alten Testaments.* I took no precise notes, and only occasionally more recently have I been able to acknowledge more accurately my indebtedness, e.g. to D. J. Wiseman (Tyndale Old Testament Commentary, 1993), S. J. DeVries (Word Bible Commentary, 1993), J. Robinson (Cambridge Bible Commentary, 1972).

The Biblical text used is that of the Revised Standard Version unless otherwise stated. It will be noted that while writing this volume I also worked with the New International Version.

INTRODUCTION

The student who has gone through the first and second books of Samuel will have read of how reluctant God was at first to set up a king over Israel in place of the temporary charismatic judges they had had from the days of Moses to Samuel. He had given way to the people's desire for such a monarchy, however, and in spite of the failure of Saul, David had pleased him perfectly when he was entrusted with this high position. In a moment of great confidence about the future of his people under this type of leadership, God therefore decided to centre his own future plans for them, and their own hope too, on a Messiah, an anointed king who would be born from the lineage of David (2 Sam. 7:12–13). Under the kingship of this future ruler there would be fulfilled the promise given under Moses, to make Israel at last, indeed,' his own possession…a kingdom of priests and a holy nation' (Ex 19:5–6). In this way too, the promises given to Abraham that his descendants would be blessed, and bring blessing to all nations of the earth (Gen. 12:2) would be fulfilled.

It obviously raised great hopes, both in the mind of king David himself and in the people who shared his faith in God, when Nathan proclaimed this promise at the peak of David's career. It seemed that great new possibilities were opening up for their nation and that they might sooner than later experience the glorious fulfilment of what their fathers such as Abraham and Moses and Joshua had longed to see. That hope was still intense as the kingdom passed from David to Solomon. Certainly tragedy had happened. David had grievously sinned, but he had shown perfect contrition and trust under God's chastisement and God had even expanded and enriched his dominions. Yet God denied him the fulfilment of one great hope. Having captured and founded the city of God, Jerusalem, he had longed to complete his service by building a temple as a dwelling place of God for ever. God had disallowed him this privilege, but had accepted his plans for it. and had promised that he would bless his son after him as he sought to crown his father's achievements by building this house of God. We are meant therefore, as we begin to read the Book of Kings to share the hope and the optimism which prevailed in the circle around David as his death approached, and as it became clear that Solomon was to be his successor. We are in a position to understand the ideals that were in the mind of the young king as he began his reign.

The first eight chapters of the book are therefore promising. Solomon is shown to respond to God with submission of heart and true faith. The temple is built, the glorious sign is given of God's presence there for ever, and the king himself is blessed. God continues to lavish his love and gifts on the man until in the tenth chapter we have a picture of him exalted to an unprecedented splendour, and a greatness acknowledged by all the surrounding nations. It is a foreshadowing of the glory of the coming Messiah.

Yet even by the time of this enacted vision, the tragedy that runs through the whole ensuing Book of Kings has already begun. God himself by this time already knows that he is working with a man who will betray his hope, and we ourselves have already been given signs that all is not well. Soon the full revelation comes suddenly and shatteringly. Solomon has turned from God to idols! He turns against God's prophet, bitterly reacts to God's chastisement, and dies as if outcast. He proves to be typical of many who will succeed him. What follows his death is ominous. His son, we discover, neglected by his father in his education, is a fool and arrogant. The nation is split, and the whole following story in the long run, on both sides, becomes one of decline and fall.

Of course, with God, nothing is irretrievable, the promise is still there, held out to be believed and grasped. And time and again throughout the whole history a fresh start is made. A child is born (cf. Isa. 7:14; 9:6). A new reign begins in hope. An Asa, a Hezekiah, a Josiah appear. God is able in the midst of the persistently recurring display of faithlessness to work with such men, to show that he remembers David and his promises, has not cast off his people, and is waiting for one who will give him the perfect trust he seeks. But none of them endures.

In the end God had to set in motion an entirely new plan in order to fulfil his purpose with this nation. They were to be punished and disciplined. They had to be made to understand the folly and hopelessness of their old ways in the midst of a long-drawn-out suffering and bitter shame. But he himself would be working with them, teaching them, healing their souls and wounds, so that in and through their sorrow and their renewed grasp of his love they could be brought to true repentance and start again. He gave them through the prophet Jeremiah the promise of a new start in which old things would pass away, and all things become new. He would meet their need by bringing about in their heart a new creation. It would all come to pass in the latter days when he would deal with them under a new covenant. (Jer. 31:31–34).

The closing chapters of Kings vividly describes the last days of the monarchy – the siege of Jerusalem, its fall, the destruction even of Solomon's great temple, the deportation of the enslaved population to Babylon.

Who was responsible for the writing, editing and issuing this book, and when did it finally appear? One suggestion is that it was written by Jeremiah. Another that we owe it to a group of scholars and thinkers who were in Babylon during the exile. The book itself tells us about the sources available at the time, from which the author or authors could have taken either information or quotations – such as e.g. the Acts of Solomon (1 Kings 11:41), and his references indicate that there were many such annals then in circulation, or in official archives about the reigns of kings available for those who desired extra information. It seems reasonable to think of a single author as being responsible for the work about the time of the exile, and, of sections being later added (e.g. 2 Kings 25:27–30), and possible editing undertaken, after the first issue.

Obviously the writer regarded the teaching of the book of Deuteronomy as of great importance. It dwells on such subjects as the dangers of misrule by a king, the ideals he should follow, the significance of the temple, and the perils of false worship. The writer of this book often can quote it at great length. He saw that the future of Israel was to be determined by whether it inherited the blessings promised in it for obedience to its laws, or the curses threatened for disobedience (Deut. 28). One of its most important laws, in his eyes, was that there should be only one centre of worship in the land (Deut. 12). It was by each king's obedience or disobedience to such teaching in this book that he finally classified them, towards the end of his account of each, as good or bad.

His constant reference to, and application of, the teaching of the book of Deuteronomy, however, need not dominate our reading of the book as we seek to find out what it has to say to us today. Within the unfolding of the history we enter a world of story, about persons like ourselves in situations that we can easily match with our own today, struggling as we ourselves have to do with the question of whether or not, and how, to obey the Word of God. The book becomes strikingly relevant to the situation faced by the Church in its struggle with modern paganism today, when the writer slows down the pace of the historical narrative to dwell, in fascinating detail, on the struggle waged by Elijah and Elisha against the falsehood and idolatry of Baal religion.

The book is written, however, not simply to analyse, explain and mourn over our human frailty and to marvel and rejoice over the faithfulness and triumph of the great prophets who warned and guided Israel. It is rather to be read as a book about God. The time of the monarchy was a tense and decisive period in his dealings with his people. The prophet Hosea lived in close communion with him during one of its crucial periods and perfectly expressed what he must have felt as he faced the fact that, in making his promise, and planning his way, he had asked too much of the human nature he was dealing with.

> How can I give you up, O Ephraim!
>   How can I hand you over, O Israel!
> How can I make you as Admah!
>   How can I treat you like Zeboim!
> My heart recoils within me,
>   my compassion grows warm and tender.
> I will not execute my fierce anger!
>   I will not again destroy Ephraim;

for I am God and not man,
    the Holy one in your midst
    and I will not come to destroy.
(Hosea 11:8–9)

The reader who enters the situations described again and again,
and yet witnesses the patience with which God holds on, will
find in these words a clue that enables us to understand the
whole book from the divine point of view.

CHAPTER I

GOD CHOOSES A KING

1 Kings 1: 1 – 53

The Narrative

David in his old age had neglected to proclaim which of his sons was to succeed him. Adonijah, the eldest surviving, unable to wait on God, tried to seize the throne in a plot which revealed his folly, self will, and inability to rule. The story shows how Nathan the prophet was inspired to intervene at the crucial moment, and to save the situation for David, Solomon, and Bathsheba.

The Question and the Candidates

One commentator on this chapter remarked that David, at this stage of his life, suffered from moral infirmity as well as from physical weakness. As we follow his career from its beginning up to the 10th chapter of 2 Samuel we are given a noble picture of the chosen king, marvellously protected and blessed by God. Apart from a few pardonable and explainable lapses he responds wholeheartedly to God's love. Then comes his sin with Bathsheba and his murder of Uriah. From this time on, though God's love never lets him go, he appears to have lost some of the joy and strength that once characterised him. His feelings of guilt impaired his ability to witness to truth and righteousness, and he was unable to become a decisive influence within his own family whom he tended to neglect. His home life was now marked by tragedy. Amnon his eldest son raped his half sister. Absolom, her brother, both in revenge, and with an eye to the throne, murdered the guilty culprit and

1

finally engaged in the rebellion that led to his own death. David, brokenhearted and more and more conscious of his own fault, marvellously bore up and continued to serve God in true repentance, yet in his old age he was as much weakened and burdened by his personal failures as well as by his earthly labours.

As he grew weaker, however, he failed to make it clear and public which of his remaining sons was to succeed him. He seems to have said enough to those around him to give the impression that he desired it to be Solomon, the son of Bathsheba. But there was sufficient indefiniteness in his expression of his will to give hope to Adonijah, an older son, with greater hereditary right, that he might be able in the midst of the uncertainty to push himself forward.

The issues were of crucial importance. The well being, indeed the future, of Israel had depended always on godly, wise and strong leadership. Its history had been prosperous and forward looking because they had at their head great men of faith and courage like Abraham, Jacob, Moses, Joshua, Samuel, and now David! The leadership question had recently been made even more acute because God had promised that there would eventually arise a successor to David's throne, greater even than David himself. A Messiah was to come, a descendant of David, under whose rule all the great promises ever given by Israel's God for themselves and for the world would be fulfilled (2 Sam. 7:11–16, 22–26). If David had not made his actual choice known, he had made it clear that his successor must seek to follow this tradition and aim at this ideal. Time and again he had described it in his Psalms (e.g. Ps.15, 18:20–24, 26:1–8, 72:1–7). David's deepest desire was, however, that his son must first of all devote his life to building a temple in which God could meet his people and glorify his name. David himself had achieved much. He had won, occupied, and built what to him was Zion, the 'holy city' in which he believed God willed to have his dwelling place among his people, at the centre of the world. He had brought the ark, the sign of God's presence into it. He had found and bought the site for the 'great house of God'. But he had been denied seeing even the foundation laid. The whole building of it (cf. I Chr. 28:2–7) was to be indeed the life-work of his son.

It is obvious that those around David's court who cared most for the future of the nation would realise that of the two it was only Solomon who gave any sign that he would accept and continue within Israel's life the tradition and hope for which David had spent his life. Adonijah could not have fitted such a pattern. Like Absalom his brother he had been allowed by his father to grow up self willed. That he was very handsome encouraged him to become vain. His lavish use of wealth and style attracted around him a court of those who loved what was superficial. Instead of having to wait on God, he had become so sure of himself that '*he exalted himself, saying, "I will be king"*' (v.5). There was not the faintest sign that this man could have achieved the task God had for David's immediate heir.

Throughout the Bible we find that the greatest servants of God, facing their life-task, had to wait till they knew themselves called by God to take it up. They invariably felt themselves unworthy and unfit to do it, and had to learn to depend on God alone for their strength. It is to Solomon's credit that though he may have known privately, that he was favoured by his father, he is seen here to make no attempt to push his claim. Even when he knew himself to be at the centre of a plot being hatched by others to manoeuvre the king and open his way to the throne, there is no trace on his part of any move to stir up support or curry his father's favour. We must take it as a sign of genuine faith and humility that he could thus wait on God to work things out his own way. Solomon certainly failed in the long run to maintain the close relationship with God which characterised the beginning of his reign, but at this stage in the affairs of the kingdom, his heart and mind were devoted fully to God's purposes.

Intrigue, Alertness, and Wisdom.

Much of this whole chapter is the rather sad story of how such a great religious issue had to be solved in a quite unworthy way. It became necessary that, following on David's negligence, the problem of who was to succeed him had finally to be solved by intrigue. Plot was followed by another plot. A cunning move by one party was met by an equally subtle counter movement by the other.

Adonijah was responsible for bringing matters to a head at a time when he thought his father had become quite incompetent of taking any counter action. He had for a time worked carefully and steadily to win strong public support for the claim he was going to make. Cashing in on his noble stature and exceptionally handsome appearance he had adopted the royal manner and style of life which he thought ordinary people would expect from a worthy king. He had begun to go about escorted by numerous chariots and outrunners. Possibly he had wanted to show that he had around him already a force strong enough to deal with any attempt by a rival faction to seize his person. He had worked with some subtlety among the king's court to test reactions to his claim. He had sounded out especially those whom he had known to be discontented with David's favouritism of people other than themselves, and he had worked on their jealousy. He had thus found two highly important sources of support. Joab, the outstanding military leader of the day, and Abiathar the retired high priest descended from Eli were on his side. Among less important officials he found enough approval to make him confident that he could bring about a coup d'état. He planned a great feast with sacrifice at a place distant enough from the centre of things to avoid interference by David's body-guard, yet central enough to be a rallying point for popular support. It was officially announced as a sheep shearing event, but he intended to make it the occasion of his being proclaimed and anointed king.

Most of the important people of the land were guests. Significantly omitted from the list of the invited, however, were Nathan, Bathsheba and '*Solomon his brother*'. At this point in the narrative we are meant to recognise a sinister element in his arrangement. Such were the customs of the time, such the tradition of fratricide in David's family, and such was the character of Adonijah, that sooner or later had the plot succeeded, Solomon's life would be in danger. This must have been in Adonijah's mind. It would have been more difficult to issue the order to kill his brother had he been present as a guest at the feast.

When Nathan, on the day of the gathering at En-rogel heard of the intention of Adonijah he had to move with desperate speed, and he planned and acted with a subtlety that outshone even that of Adonijah. He had the advantage of the presence of the king and needed only to decide on the best way immediately to alert and arouse David. But the king had become distant and moody at this time of his life and he had to be careful. He cleared the way for his own approach by first sending in Bathsheba, once David's favourite wife, with a story certain to awaken and alarm him. No doubt it was well rehearsed. Why had he allowed what was going on? Did he realise that now his own life, and the life of Solomon, were now in dire danger? Did he not remember the hope he had given her that Solomon would be king? Why had he not warned her of his change of mind? How could he have treated her thus? (vv. 17 – 21).

David had not recovered from the shock of this genuinely emotional outburst when the man he had always most needed in a crisis (cf. 2 Sam. 7:3–4; 12:1) was there at the door waiting for the crucial moment. Nathan showed further skill and wisdom in employing tactics quite in contrast to those he had suggested to Bathsheba. He knew that the king had a sensitive conscience when he was justly and bluntly accused for failure in duty. He judged it was now time to face him squarely with his recent neglect of his realm. He challenged him about his failure to think out the possible effects of his indecision. Did he really mean what was about to happen when he had declared Adonijah his successor? Why had he done this and left all his loyal friends in ignorance? (vv. 24–27). The central thrust in the whole of the accusation was: why had he misled Bathsheba when he had told her he wanted Solomon?

The whole experience of being thus touched, aroused and rebuked suddenly and completely changed David's mood and attitude. God had spoken to him again, clearly and mercifully! He was grateful and repentant. He thanked God that through Nathan and Bathsheba, he had been rescued from both his troubles, and himself, and brought back into God's service (vv. 29–30). He could start again with God, and he lost no time in assuming command. His orders were precise and thorough, and even before Adonijah had time to raise his standard at En-rogel,

Solomon was crowned. The trumpets were sounded and all streets of the city resounded again and again with cheering.

We must give full credit to Nathan for his alertness. He realised that God had placed him in a key position in this very acute and fateful situation. He had to be continually on the watch against those whose ways were a danger to truth. He had to take full responsibility in the crisis, to begin to act alone.

We have also to admire the way he did it. Of all the parables of Jesus, one most difficult to understand is about the manager of an estate whom Jesus praised because in a crisis he saved himself from utter ruin by a very dubious series of financial transactions. Jesus held him up for our admiration, not because of his roguery, but because of the sheer cleverness he showed in preparing to see himself successfully through all his coming problems. At the end of the story Jesus expresses the hope that his own followers, in his service, might prove themselves as wise as this rascal. 'The master commended the dishonest manager, because he had acted shrewdly' (Luke 16:8, N.I.V.). Jesus desired to find in the activity of his disciples the same watchfulness, boldness, energy, and (if need be) subtlety, as was shown by the man in the parable, and he lamented that too often he found it lacking. 'For the people of this world are more shrewd in dealing with their own kind than are the people of the light' (Luke 16:9). Jesus must have admired, and perhaps learned from, Nathan, for much of his teaching derived from what he learned from the Old Testament.

We have refrained from calling Nathan's behaviour 'intrigue'. It did not require to be covered up from the public. Abishag obviously remained in the room all the time as a witness! Moreover, he was not seeking his own advancement but only that of the kingdom of God in Israel. We have therefore called it 'wisdom' – a wisdom that can find its inspiration in God himself. Nathan is here a perfect example of the ideal Jesus set before his disciples when he said: 'Be wise as serpents and innocent as doves' (Matt. 10:16).

'God works all things together for good' (Romans 8:28)

David gives us the final clue to the interpretation of this

incident in the words he spoke as he was reviewing , at the end
of the day, everything that had happened: '*Praise be to the Lord,
the God of Israel, who has allowed my eyes to see a successor on my
throne today*' (v. 48, N.I.V.). It had been a decisive day for the
future of the kingdom of God. A miracle had taken place to
change radically both his own outlook and his whole situation!

Yet God had made no spectacularly miraculous intervention
in human affairs. He had not struck Adonijah down with any
sudden illness nor had he sent a bolt of warning lightning
from heaven to spoil his celebration. At the right time, and in
the right situation he had simply inspired minds with thoughts
that moved them on, and given the exact words that were
required to turn events in the right direction. Moreover in
everything that had brought about the miracle he had done
his work in a quite unnoticed way, and it was only in the end
that David's own people had been able to marvel at what had
been achieved. In everything that each character had done,
whether intended for good or evil, God had been actively at
work controlling everything that happened so that his will was
eventually and triumphantly done.

We are reminded in this incident of how marvellously God
moved human family affairs in a very similar situation earlier
in Israel's history. Isaac and Rebekah had to decide which of
their two sons, Esau or Jacob, should become the heir to the
'blessing' that Isaac had to pass on from his father Abraham.
Here within the family circle there had been, and continued
to be, division, intrigue, jealous rivalry, and a strange
unwillingness to consult with and submit to God. Yet God had
his way. Isaac had to be tricked into giving the blessing to Jacob,
the one God had chosen. He felt inspired by God, as he did
so, imagining that he was giving it to Esau! In the end he had
to acknowledge, as David did in this present incident, that God
had had full control of him, even in this disobedient mood, to
work his own perfect will and he acknowledged it with thankful
resignation: 'Yes, and he shall be blessed'! (Gen. 27:33)

It is worth our while, in our present case, to go over the
story and trace more exactly the way it happened. We are meant
to notice, for instance, that it was Adonijah who did all the
clever planning, and he was allowed to move to the brink of
success. God, indeed, seemed to go about his affairs haphazardly

and to allow things to drift to the verge of disaster. Yet, in the way it happened, it is brought out very clearly that on the side of those who supported Solomon there was healthy willingness to wait for God himself to show his will and take action. We cannot doubt that in the decisive moments when they pled with the king they were praying. The current saying may have been in their minds: 'The king's heart is in the hand of the Lord: he directs it like a watercourse wherever he pleases' (Prov. 21:1, N.I.V.).

Adonijah's fiasco was as providentially inspired and controlled as were these last minute interventions at the king's sick-bed, and it proved to be his undoing. If he had only waited a little longer, the king might have passed away with nothing decided, and he could easily have won his way to the throne — for he had more legal right than his brother. Moreover he had on his side the most powerful military leader in the land with important supporters. Are we not meant to understand that it was through a God-given anxiety that he was induced to make this fatal mistake, and to marvel at the result of his being spurred on to show his hand so prematurely? In making his claim he exposed so clearly his vanity and inability to rule in place of his father that there could never remain in any fair - minded person's thought, any suspicion that God had not been wise in the choice of Solomon.

We are meant too, to observe how in the very moment of their expected triumph the over ambitious conspirators all heard faintly in the distance, but clearly and unmistakably, as if from God, the sound of the approaching judgement and doom. It is characteristic of the way God deals with opposition to his rule that he often allows his opponents full scope to express what is in their minds and hearts so that there may be no doubt that in the end they deserved the punishment they received. He thus allows evil movements often to break out and ripen in order to show their true nature before they are finally crushed. This is why the way he deals with evil often seems perplexingly lax to those who want to see it more immediately crushed. Yet when the hour of the final demise of an evil movement within earth's history finally comes, he often brings about its fall in a tellingly dramatic way as here in our story, so that those who are around to observe it, may not escape the lesson that God is at work.

Points for Further Thought and Discussion

The pushing self-advertisement, and self-confident ambition, of Adonijah are, in this particular story, regarded as disqualifying him for success in the service of God. Is this in accord with the teaching of the Bible generally? If so, are we meant to regard this warning as relevant to our life in the world today?

Do we today, like David, by our failure to take action, and to make our priorities in the way of life clear, tend to encourage those around us to think we approve even of falsehood and evil?

Can you think of instances in the Bible, and in human history, when God changed the whole human situation by inspiring one key individual to speak and act? Might we not often find ourselves within our circle of family and friends in the position of Nathan?

Some commentators suggest that David had never really expressed his preference for Solomon, and that Bathsheba and Nathan were 'conning' him in suggesting this. Can you think of instances, in Church and personal life today, when our attempts at being 'wise' simply reveal that we are 'worldly' – because we are not 'as innocent as doves' (cf. Matt. 10:16)?

We are often perplexed by the scope to grow and flourish that God seems often to give to evil movements and forces in history. Might it not be that, as with Adonijah, he allows evil to express and expose itself before it is finally judged? Do we find in the judgement given to evil in the cross, a full and clear expression of this way of working?

Notes

Abishag
It was commonly believed from primitive times that such close contact with the body of Abishag could pass on to the

king not only physical warmth but also a curative vitality which could help to restore his waning health. This task was assigned to her as well as being his nurse and attendant.

The Origin of 1 Kings 1 and 2

The first two chapters of 1 Kings are obviously the closing part of a historical account of the latter years of David's reign in Jerusalem which begins at 2 Samuel chapter 9. These chapters tell one continuous story and were all written by the same author who was obviously closely informed about what was taking place within David's court and family circles. He writes as if he himself were an intimate observer of what he is reporting. It is acknowledged that his work is a 'skilful product of literary genius'. He gives us an unforgettable and poignant account of David's sin with Bathsheba, and how it was purged. He dwells especially on the vengeful and lustful passion, the selfish ambition and pride, that brought about the deadly conflict between David's sons, Amnon and Absalom, resulting finally in the rebellion and death of Absalom. The story now closes with the contest between Adonijah and Solomon. Because such rivalry between David's sons is its central theme, the history is often called 'the Succession Narrative'.

CHAPTER II

SOLOMON BECOMES 'ESTABLISHED'

1 Kings 2 : 1 – 46

The Narrative

After a period of renewed vigour, David blessed Solomon from his death-bed and warned him. His conscience made him blame himself for neglecting to crush those who had been a threat to his realm, and he counselled Solomon to lose no time. Providentially Solomon needed to take no initiative. Adonijah, now his worst enemy, took a false and devious step, and the others destroyed themselves in acts that revealed their folly and fear. We again can see the hand of God providentially at work.

Renewal, Resignation and Hope

The sharp word spoken by Nathan to David to arouse him to action in the crisis caused by Adonijah's rebellion had more than a momentary effect. According to the account in Chronicles (1 Chron. 28–29), he was delivered entirely from his mood of withdrawal and hesitation. No longer willing to accept wrecked hopes or shattered ideals he became again in spirit the David he had been for God in his early days, and he was granted a remarkable, if short, period of mental alertness and physical vigour.

The transformation was marvellous. The old king was able, by himself, to confirm his choice before a public gathering at Jerusalem. He even 'rose to his feet' and was given the strength to speak. He surveyed his hopes and plans for the nation's future. He proclaimed Solomon as his successor, pled for his

11

support, charged him especially with the building of the temple and endowed him with his wealth for this purpose. In his charge he dwelt on the responsibility of privilege: 'and you, Solomon, my son acknowledge the God of your father, and serve him with a whole heart and a willing mind, for the Lord searches all hearts and understands every plan and thought. If you seek him he will be found by you; but if you forsake him he will cast you off for ever. Take heed now for the Lord has chosen you to build a house for the sanctuary. Be strong and do it' (1 Chron. 28:9–10).

Now, alone with Solomon, he can no doubt more freely and intimately express his feelings. Certainly he is now more resigned and submissive. His words, '*I am about to go the way of all the earth*' (v. 2) are a frank admission that his life in full measure has been beset by weakness, and marked by the tragic occurrences which seem at times to make death a fitting end to our human span of life. Many Old Testament scholars tell us that hope of life after death would be no help to him. They affirm that he must have shared the prevalent belief of his time, that death led to a rather colourless and gloomy existence in a place called Sheol (see note). This is a view he seems to express in what he says about Joab and Shimei (vv. 6, 9).

Yet we need not take it for granted that he had no greater expectation about his own future than such a doctrine could have given him. We are justified in believing that, even at this moment, though his mind may have been bound and restricted by such traditional thoughts, there was an element in his experience which lifted him in hope and vision far above the level down to which mere tradition would have dragged him. Though he was facing this mysterious and dreaded journey, '*the way of all the earth*', he knew he was being taken through it in the hands of an abundantly good and powerful God in whose abiding fellowship he has experienced a marvellous inner resurrection. This God was then, for David, as we know him to be for ourselves, the God of hope (Rom. 15:13). That hope was certainly centred chiefly on what was to happen within this earth's history for the people of Israel. At that time it meant the fulfilment of God's promises of being blessed and becoming a blessing to all nations (Gen.12:2–3). For the individual at that time it meant primarily companionship and prosperity during the allotted span of earthly life. David is here passing on such earthly hope to Solomon. He is reminding him that the promise given him years ago by Nathan would guarantee the earthly future of his house and line as they continued from generation to generation to follow on his throne in expectation of a promised Messiah.

Yet as he seeks to pass on this earthly hope by the power of God to his son, David is not, himself, unaffected by what he is doing. His mood is of peaceful commitment. He is yielding himself not in depressed resignation to a dismal fate but in triumphant trust that the grace of God, which has so gloriously crowned all his efforts for Israel, will somehow be with him still as he moves beyond the earthly scene. It is our belief that earlier in his life, as his mind dwelt on the closeness of his own relationship with God, David gave more clear expression to the hope that such a bond could not be interrupted by death. The sixteenth Psalm, for instance, expresses in a mood of serene confidence the hope that God must have something better for him than a mere 'Sheol' (cf. Ps. 16:8–11). Possibly at this final moment he was not able to rise again to the certainty that he then expressed. Yet he is again the David who, in his younger days, could give such expression to the wistful hope before God that not even death could separate him from his love. The 'doctrine of a future life' says one Old Testament scholar 'came gradually and through long struggles, and was only fully realised when Christ annulled death, and brought life and immortality to light through the Gospel' (2 Tim.1:10). David, here, we believe, was beginning on the way towards it.

The Blessed Way of Life

In the days of the patriarchs it was believed that the solemn words spoken by a father especially when he was at the point of death could be powerful in their effect on his children. Both Isaac and Jacob, for instance, firmly believed that the blessings and future promises with which God had endowed their family line through Abraham could be effectively passed on to their chosen son through such a death-bed utterance (cf. Gen.27:27, 33; 49:1, 8–10). It is our belief that king David now at the hour of his death facing his son, remembered these stories of Israel's past tradition, and desired that his last words might in the same way be both memorable and powerful. His prime concern is that the promise (and the blessing contained in it) which has so dominated his life since it was given to him by Nathan (cf. 2 Sam. 7:12), should now take over Solomon's heart and mind, inspire and direct his actions, and thus move on into history towards its ultimate glorious fulfilment. He is here blessing his son in order '*that the Lord may establish his word which he spoke concerning me*' (v. 4). The inheritance of the blessing is to be ensured for the future as each generation of David's family follows the way of life, which it pleased God to find in David himself.

In describing his way of life David mentions first the keeping of the '*law of Moses*' (v. 3). He himself had loved the law. It had made God's will for his life clear and simple. It had been his delight to fulfil it. It had been his salvation to find that when he broke it, it also enabled him to find forgiveness and the way to put his life right again. He is passing on the promise, when he is passing on the law. The keeping of the law had been a framework in which a deep and living relationship with God himself had been made possible and had found expression. It had brought him near to God in his sanctuary where he had beheld God's 'face' and 'gazed upon his beauty' (Ps. 27:4, 7–9), and had been able to express his love to him.

David's word to his descendants, however, finds its climax in God's claim that they '*walk before me in faithfulness with all their heart and soul*' (v. 4). He is reminding them of God's command to Abraham: 'walk before me, and be blameless' (Gen. 17:1). In much of the ordinary routine of their daily lives they would have to live by faith and faithfulness (cf. Hab. 2:4) rather than by the intimately felt experience of God's nearness. There would be distance enough between them and himself to leave them free to choose their own path of life and to ensure that the devotion they gave to him was the outflow of a deep and steady personal commitment of heart and will to him (cf. John 16:7). Yet they would have the certainty that he was indeed 'above' and that they were 'before him'. He was there watching over their ways and their struggles, ready to hear, help and guide both in daily and dire need. What mattered most was that they should never be diverted by personal suffering or by the threat of an enemy, or ever begin to walk merely before the public opinion of people or the flattery of their friends.

What it meant to please God under the Old Covenant, and to become the true heirs of the great promises given by God to Israel could not have been put more clearly and more attractively than in this death-bed charge by David. He himself had kept the faith in this way, and even as he passed on the blessing, he looked forward with confidence that the promise given to him by God could not fail: 'Your house and your kingdom shall be made sure for ever before me; your throne shall be established for ever' (2 Sam. 7:16).

The Book of Kings tells the story of dismal failure of king after king, even the best of them, to walk wholeheartedly in such a way '*before*' God. God was patient. He held on to his promise long after it had become obvious that the earthly line of royal kings, for which David had such hope, had to come to an end in shame, wretchedness and tragedy. And even then, as the last of David's successors was removed from his earthly throne into captivity, a vision of hope was given to one of the great prophets of that day. It was of a new way of life under a new covenant: 'I will put my law in their minds and write it on their hearts. ... they will all know me from the least of them to the greatest.... and I will make a righteous Branch sprout from David's line; he will do what is just and right in the land (Jer. 31:33–34; 33:15, N.I.V.).

Threat and Concern

What possessed David that, immediately after such an impressive last word, his mood, and the tone and theme of what he said, should seem to change so drastically? The tendency to a swift change of mood was one of his weaknesses, and here, tragically, he shifted his attention too suddenly and completely from the thought of God's promises to the critical state of affairs that he was now leaving behind him in Israel, and his hope tended to give way before deep concern.

Possibly some uncertainty about the character of Solomon
had already caused him a measure of anxiety. He had wondered
whether he would have the wisdom and steadfastness to be
able to cope. He himself had been able to serve God faithfully
in face of continual difficulties because by the grace of God he
had been made strong when nearly everyone else around him
had been weak. Was Solomon conscious enough of this source
of strength? The exhortation to 'be strong' had been uttered
as an urgent warning. More disturbing thoughts now flooded
into his mind. Certain affairs, indeed, seemed to threaten the
very fulfilment of the promise itself. The realisation that Joab
had become a leader in the faction opposing Solomon
especially troubled his conscience. Joab had been a criminal
who had treacherously murdered two noble men without any
cause, and he, David the king, had been too weak to bring
him to justice. He firmly believed that the guilt of this
unpunished murder was bound, unless it was purged, to bring
disaster on the kingdom. Solomon must now be urged to do
what alone could save the situation.

It was the same kind of motive which lay behind his desire
to settle the case of Shimei. This man had uttered a deadly
curse on David and his house (2 Sam. 16:1–13). The potency
of this invective could, he felt, be removed only by the death
of the one who uttered it. David at the time he had been
subjected to it had foolishly sworn that he would take no
counteraction because his mind had been too preoccupied by
his temporary troubles. But Solomon must now undertake to
make good his failure.

It is to be regretted that David's language in giving this
charge to his son can be interpreted too easily as if he were
expressing a desire for revenge against two personal enemies
(see note). We believe that it was his desire for the future
Kingdom of God that gave force to his zeal to crush what
opposed God's kingdom. He was, of course, also giving
expression to his own bad conscience in his advice to Solomon.
He was vexed that he himself had failed during his reign to
carry out the purge. He had never felt quite able to control
Joab, and he had been foolish in his treatment of Shimei. In
his call to Solomon to '*show yourself a man*' it is possible to trace
a note of regret that he himself at times had become

unmanned, and had lacked the courage to deal decisively with such potential hindrances to progress. It is to be noted that in his appeal to the young king he is calling not for revenge but for wisdom (vv. 6, 9). He was certain that with such men given freedom, Solomon himself might be in danger, and his kingdom would lack the peace and stability needed for the kind of work he had to do. Therefore he urged Solomon to be ruthless. There must be no hesitation or compunction. He pleads for blood to be shed.

A bungalow dweller in India, when one of the great rivers was in flood, found himself in his bungalow garden on a small island with wide surrounding fields of water. And there in the water swimming towards him he saw a large and beautiful tiger. As it reached his refuge it seemed relieved and fawning, and he was tempted to welcome it. But wisdom prevailed and he took his gun and shot it dead. Only with such ruthlessness could Solomon himself fulfil God's purpose. He must encourage around him only those whom he could absolutely trust.

The Purge and Providence

Solomon's swiftness of action in response to David's death-bed charge tends to give the impression that he was abusing his newly given power and that there was a streak of ruthless cruelty in his own make up. There is, however, no evidence from any other aspect of his early life for such a view. There was a more obvious cause. Solomon revered his father, recognised the wisdom of his death-bed advice and the dangers to which he had been alerted, and accepted his orders without question as a Word of God.

We believe that his decision to execute Adonijah was understandably forced upon him by an act of brazen self destructive folly on the latter's part. Abishag, after the death of David , had an important status as a concubine of the dead king, and Adonijah's desire for her hand was inevitably to be interpreted as the expression of lurking ambition towards the throne. His raising of the matter after being ordered to keep in retirement showed open contempt for his brother. His decision to make his approach in a roundabout way through Bathsheba rather than directly to Solomon was evidence that he was prepared to transact important business behind the king's back. We can understand that Solomon felt cornered and humiliated and deeply shocked when Bathsheba made her '*small request*' (v. 20). Even his mother had been deceived and wholly won over by this cunning smoothness! How could he begin to reign in peace when around his very throne a treacherous brother, with a strong faction behind him, was beginning already to show his hand? His father's words were still there, and powerful in his mind, 'Be strong!' and Be wise!'. It was under his influence that he made his fateful decision. Again we can, if we will, see it as providential that God allowed Adonijah's folly to express itself a second time so soon and so clearly, to bring about his downfall.

Whatever distaste Solomon may have had for the fateful course he was now to follow was suddenly overcome. He felt that here and now he must begin to put in action the policy and plan his father had so powerfully urged. Among those by whom he felt endangered was Abiathar the priest who had agreed to anoint Adonijah. Obviously he did not want on his hands the blood of a priest who had once loyally served his father, but even as he banished him he declared him guilty and under the sentence of death. Making this sentence known was an intended warning to Joab of what was in his mind, and Joab understood. Astonishingly the strong man of whose rebuke even David had once been afraid, suddenly became paralysed with fear, and fled defenceless to an altar, in the temporary tabernacle which had been erected in Jerusalem to house the ark. There was a law (cf. Exod. 21:12–13) which offered freedom to anyone who had unintentionally killed another, and then fled in this way to a sanctuary. But Joab's crime was in Solomon's eyes that of quite intentional murder (cf. 2 Sam. 3:27; 20:9–10) and he reckoned that Joab had admitted his guilt clearly enough to justify his execution.

It was to Solomon's credit that he hesitated to carry out his father's advice immediately and slay Shimei. He simply at first restricted his movements to prevent him from fomenting any trouble in parts of the country that were open to his influence. Shimei could have lived his life out in quietness, but death was to be the penalty for ignoring the king's orders. After three years he courted the very execution which Solomon had sought to avoid. It is noted by the narrator that it was only after he too was dead that '*the kingdom was established in the hand of Solomon*' (v. 46).

It is a remarkable feature in this whole series of events that those whom Solomon executed, themselves either gave him justifiable cause for the action he took, or provoked him to an action he might not have otherwise taken. As we read through this whole series of events we are meant to note that they happened by the providence of God rather than by any deliberately made plan of Solomon.

If Adonijah, for example, had waited in quietness, affairs in Israel were so delicately poised that it might indeed have been very difficult for Solomon to shoulder responsibility for the action he felt justified in taking. Shimei too could have lived on to be a continual threat to Solomon's peace. Joab declared his own guilt before Solomon directly confronted him. The final fate in each case was brought about by a stupidity of mind that made each court his own destruction. It is not surprising that commentators at this point quote the old adage: 'Whom the gods destroy, they first make mad.'

Points for Further Thought and Discussion

Has our own failure to believe in the blessedness and goodness of the life to come anything to do with our tendency to depression and our lack of moral zeal?

We have argued that it was because David had such great hope for Solomon's future, that he was so anxiously concerned about the evils that might hinder its fulfilment. Can Christian hope today be genuine if it is not accompanied by concern about its fulfilment? In what ways should such concern find expression?

Do we ourselves sometimes fail both to give a clear witness to our faith, and to attempt to change the circumstances around us, because, like David, we overestimate the strength of those who oppose our faith and way of life ?

Do we ourselves fail by being too lenient – with ourselves, towards our friends, within our family circle? If Church life is to be healthy can we avoid offending people by open criticism or rebuke? Do you think that if our national life is to be restored to health, we need a more severe treatment of offenders?

A recent conservative commentator on Kings suggests that, even though God overruled his actions, Solomon was nevertheless unwise in bringing about the purge so zealously because 'it led to divisions which lasted through the Davidic dynasty'. Do you agree? Read Jesus' advice to those who wanted to separate the tares from the wheat before the harvest (Matt. 13:29). Does this apply here?

Notes

Life After Death in the Old Testament
As we read through the Old Testament following the guidance of some scholarly commentators it appears that, especially in the earliest centuries, the great majority of God's people believed that, even though life in this world under the providence and love of God could be full of blessing and joy, there was nothing of such

grace and goodness to look forward to in the next world. The prevalent view, we are told, was that death ushered all of us into a place called 'Sheol' – an underworld where though there is no torment or retribution, silence and darkness prevail. and God is not remembered and praised (cf. Ps. 6:5; 30:9; 88:11; 115:17; Job 10:21). The assertion is sometimes made that only in a few passages of late origin do we have a clear statement in the Old Testament of a resurrection of the dead (in Isa. 26:19; Dan. 12:2–3).

We ourselves in the above exposition have raised questions about such conclusions. Our Lord himself pointed out that the word: 'I am the God of Abraham, of Isaac and Jacob' (Matt. 22:32) was spoken by God to Moses long after the three patriarchs had died. This implies that the thought of a future glory for those who served God was there for the taking. It was certainly taken, for example, by the author of Psalm 73 who found great consolation in it when he was perplexed by the problem of apparent unjust suffering (cf. vv. 23–25). The Psalmists often protest against the thought of Sheol as their fate, (Ps. 55:15–17; cf. also Ps. 49:15; 86:13). We regard it as significant that God 'took' Enoch, the man who 'walked with him' (Gen. 5:24), sparing him the very experience of dying so that his loving relationship with the man might not be interrupted.

David's Advice on Joab
We can find mixed motives in David's wish to see Joab removed from his place of influence. Joab had known how deeply it would grieve David when he deliberately killed Absalom, and the king had found him often over-zealous and unreliable in the leadership with which he had been entrusted. Commentators on this passage have accused David of 'black perfidy' and 'bloodthirsty desire for revenge'. We believe, however, that the king was genuinely and strongly motivated by the superstition he here professed. On one occasion, undoubtedly against his personal desire (cf. 2 Sam. 9:1), he slaughtered sons of Saul because he had become sincerely convinced that a crime of their father's had not been purged (2 Sam. 21). We agree with Skinner who asks us at this point to think of the chivalrous magnanimity of David's character: 'David was after all a child of his age liable to be swayed by the superstitious beliefs then prevalent which quenched his nobler impulses and made ideal ethical conduct impossible'.

CHAPTER III

SOLOMON ACCEPTED, TESTED AND CONFIRMED
1 Kings 3:1–28

The Narrative

> We are assured here that, in spite of excusable
> compromise, Solomon at the beginning of his reign 'loved
> the Lord'. In a prayer inspired by a dream-vision given to
> him one night, he revealed that his first concern in life
> was to be given wisdom and to rule well. God, greatly
> pleased, promised him also wealth and fame. Following
> this promise we are given a remarkable instance of the
> gift that brought him such fame.

The Man before God

The account we have been given so far of Solomon's rise to
the throne and his establishment in power has been mainly
factual. Though it has been remarkably detailed, interesting,
and written by a close observer of events, the writer has given
us no hint of the motives Solomon himself might have had in
the attitude he adopted, or the actions he took. We have been
left to make our own judgement on his character.

Solomon, too, has managed to hide his feelings and motives.
Like too many of us in the Church and public life today there
is always in him a tendency to hide the person behind the
official attitude he adopts.

We ourselves have so far given him the benefit of the doubt,
and have put a favourable interpretation on what we have read
of him. Yet other commentators do not share our view and
hint that Solomon was cunning and bloodthirsty (see note).

22

This present chapter, we believe, justifies the interpretation we have so far taken of his actions. It reveals him as single minded and genuine towards God. This is a view that we must maintain until, as later happens, a tragic inexplicable change has occurred.

Readers are sometimes troubled by two apparent faults which are mentioned at the beginning of our present chapter. The first is Solomon's marriage to the daughter of Pharaoh, king of Egypt. The law of God did not, however forbid the marriage of the men of Israel to foreign wives, but only to those of Canaanite origin. This marriage was understandable. Israel had by this time expanded to become an important neighbour of Egypt and David himself would probably have approved of such an expedient political move. Though Solomon's foreign wives later become a danger to him this one need not have been followed by so many. The only real fault mentioned in this chapter is that he chose the '*high place*' at Gibeon as a place of worship. We have to note that he is immediately excused for doing so, because the alternative site at Jerusalem did not offer him the scope he required fully to express his devotion to the Lord. That devotion found its expression in a great day of celebration when a thousand burnt offerings were made.

It was at night, immediately after this celebration that '*The Lord appeared to Solomon in a dream*' (v. 5). This happening was decisive in the career of the young king. It was a sign of God's approval of his way. He had read the heart, and accepted the man and his devotion, as well as the sacrifice. 'A dream like Solomon's, says one commentator, does not happen when the day has been spent in revelling' It is the 'pure in heart' who see God (Matt. 5:8).

The fact that such a vision was given, is full of promise for the future of this monarchy. 'Blessed are those you choose and bring near' (Ps. 65:4, N.I.V.). Here is a new openness to God's presence which can be the beginning of a continually deepening friendship between God and Solomon. God has destined him for a service that is to be fruitful and lasting (John 15: 16). We are justified in comparing what happened at this stage in Solomon's life to one of these renewing experiences which can come to people today within the Church – not through any dream and not through a 'spectacular' opening of the heavens, but rather through one of these no less powerful experiences of hearing the Word of God, and seeing what it speaks about, which Jesus insisted should take place repeatedly among us (cf. Matt.13:16–17; John 1:51).

'Ask for whatever you want me to give you'

The second Psalm was used at the anointing and installation of kings in Israel, and it could possibly have been composed for the official coronation of Solomon himself. In it the king is called to live in confidence before God as a son before a father, and he is to find the strength and wisdom to rule successfully by continual asking and receiving:

> He said to me, 'You are my Son;
>   today I have become your Father.
> Ask of me, and I will make the nations your inheritance,
>   the ends of the earth your possession.' (vv. 7–8, N.I.V.)

It is significant that God initiated Solomon's new life with himself by saying 'Ask'. This is the most important feature of the new relationship into which God is seeking to lift him. He will have success only if he depends wholly on what comes to him from God and continually and trustfully asks for what God is ready to give him.

In the request that he should 'ask', God is putting Solomon under a test. The kind of man he is will be revealed in his answer. It is important that God should hear his personally-given decision. How far could he trust this man? What burden could he lay on him? Was he fully aware of his responsibility? How clear was his vision of the task? How capable was he of making use of the great gifts God was now ready to give him in order to equip him? Could he be trusted not to abuse a position and power which no leader of Israel had ever before been given?

It was a severe test. It was put to Solomon in abrupt suddenness with no prior hint that it was to be given. The answer was demanded there and then without meditation or attempt at dress rehearsal – no cover up of what was there in the heart! It is significant, too, that it was put under dream conditions, away from the inhibitions and conventions of the surrounding world that so often keep us from being or revealing our true selves.

The confession '*I am but a little child*' (v. 7) reveals the sense of the urgent need out of which Solomon gave God the answer he was seeking, '*Give thy servant an understanding mind to govern thy people, that I may discern between good and evil*' (v. 9). The responsibility he most dreaded in the task to which he had been called was that of being the judge of those who were brought before him for his verdict. One of his own proverbs ran, 'Inspired decisions are on the lips of a king; his mouth does not sin in judgement' (Pr. 16:10). He knew well how often scandals and tragedies occur in civil life because those who administer the law are short sighted and easily perverted. But he believed that the God of Israel was willing to be there, presiding over his own people's destiny, always ready to vindicate the innocent, to expose the wicked and to watch over the course of events. The Lord himself could unerringly read the heart and was ready to share his wisdom with those who sought his help in the task of reflecting his justice among men. Solomon sought therefore this gift from God – an insight from above. He wanted something more than mere worldly prudence, or the shrewdness and tact that come from long human experience. He prays for the divine power to identify the good and evil in every human situation however complex and confused.

The pleasure God took in Solomon's reply was expressed in an immediate series of gratuitous promises all with the design of assuring that his reign would indeed become a fitting complement to the marvellous reign of David himself. This was a great moment not only for Solomon but also for the whole future of Israel itself. David, in his kingship and person had already managed to reveal in this world some faint traces of the glory and kingship of the future Messiah, and it had been God's purpose that within David's future earthly line of kings more was to be shown than had appeared even in David himself. God, faced by this young and ardent worshipper made the decision that he should be the one to complete the pattern. He would become to the whole world not only an example of the wisdom and justice of the coming eternal Messiah but he would also reflect even in his person, court, and earthly dominion, something of his riches and honour. Solomon was there and then promised that God would make him such a king – so *'that in your lifetime you will have no equal'* (v. 13 N.I.V.) and he would prosper in living it out if *'you walk in my ways and obey my statutes'* (v. 14).

Before moving on we must not become so taken up by the uniqueness of what was happening within the history of Israel that we fail to overhear the important question which this incident puts to each of us at the level of our personal lives. It comes to us as we, too, face the call and challenge of God: 'Ask what I shall give you!' As a recent commentator has put it, 'God's giving will correspond to Solomon's asking. There are no limits except those that our own faith imposes. Solomon can never ask more than God is willing to give. Yet if God is to give Solomon must ask, and he will be tested by what he asks for. Our requests reveal what sort of persons we are.' (De Vries)

Of course it is Jesus himself who has taught us unforgettably that since God is our Father we can have confidence in our asking. He has enabled us, too, to receive in our hearts the same spirit of sonship as he himself had so that we become bold and even familiar in our asking. It is he who has shown us through his life on earth how to live always completely dependent on what we ask for. And he has made us kings and priests to God! Does his teaching not challenge us even more searchingly than God challenged Solomon? 'Ask, and it will be given to you; seek and you will find; knock and the door will be opened to you' (Matt. 7:7 N.I.V.). And does he not reproach us that we ask so little?

The Sign

This chapter comes to its climax in the story of a particular case which was soon brought before Solomon – the case of two prostitutes in their dispute over a child. – It was a case of extreme difficulty for there were no witnesses, and each pled her case eloquently.

Scholars tell us that similar stories of astonishing skill being shown in cases of judgement are to be found in the old religious

and secular traditions of other lands (see note). They suggest
that this story was imported into Israel's history from some
such tradition and was attached here to the biblical record in
order to illustrate the wisdom of Solomon. The existence of
other stories, however, need not cast doubt on the actual
historicity of this one. This case in Israel was regarded by his
own people as a convincing sign that the king was indeed a
man of God. The story, while it is intensely human, has features
which are unique to Israel and, within its Old Testament setting,
a meaning can be found in it, which it will not readily yield in
any other context.

   We can best explain the meaning if we first remind the
reader of one of the central features of the history of the people
of God. Israel was a people whom God had especially chosen
for a great purpose. We find God constantly at work in the
midst, giving them his presence, shining the light of his truth
into their minds through chosen teachers, bringing them
under his laws, taking them under his care and subjecting them
to his providential discipline. Yet, strangely, as the generations
pass and the truth becomes more full, clear and undeniable,
there appears within this favoured nation a gradually growing
and hardening opposition to the light – a resistance that seeks
even to quench it. It is this age long resistance of our humanity
to God's love and truth that Jesus finally and decisively
encounters, exposes and overcomes in his life, death and
resurrection. But it was there in humanity from the time of
the fall, and it never ceased to mark the life of the people of
God. Throughout the Bible therefore, we can discern, time
and again, the division of the men and women of Israel into
those who in the course of time under his providence seem to
allow themselves to become hardened against him and their
fellow beings, and those who under the same kind of
providence yield in love to him and to the service of others.
Cain and Abel, Esau and Jacob, Saul and David are typical
examples.

   Here among these two women the same process is taking
place. Each has fallen low in earthly status. They are rejected
by society. Only God can help them. Life can have no meaning
or future for them except by a miracle that he alone can work,
if in their desperation they turn to him. One woman has,

however given herself up to bitter self centredness. After the death of her child she has lost all hope for her own future and has abandoned herself to the task of wrecking life for others. She will find satisfaction now only if she can drag down her neighbour into her own helplessness even if it costs the slaughter of an innocent child. The other woman is genuine in heart, even though she has sunk as low in her social condition as her grim and tragic neighbour.

She has hope. She believes that life has true worth and is beginning to have new thoughts about it. In her desperate anxiety she is now looking to God's all seeing wisdom to vindicate her, but she is prepared, and is offering, to pay the greatest sacrifice she is capable of giving if only her child can live.

Solomon in his judgement shows deep insight into what is taking place under God's grace in his realm. It is a remarkable feature of the case that as he passes judgement he also at the same time clearly exposes the sinister and infinitely cruel nature of the evil desire exposed in the self condemned woman. As he vindicates the other, moreover, he reveals that in the depths of human sadness and sorrow there can arise a readiness to respond and cling to the justice, hope, and life that can come from no other source than God himself. Exposure and separation! Do we not find here, taking place under the judgement of Solomon, the same division as took place finally and decisively when Jesus himself came and lived and taught among us? To do this was not the chief purpose of his coming, but it happened (John 3:17). When he went about among us, working and appealing, the deep division that had prevailed below the surface of things was made clear. And when he comes again it will be finally to 'bring to light what is hidden in darkness' and 'to expose the motives of the hearts' (I Cor. 4:5; Matt. 25:32; Luke 2:34–35).

Indeed through this story we find our mind drawn to Christ on his Cross. There, of the two thieves, we see one hurling insults at life and goodness itself, while we see the other seeking salvation from the same source. We see, too, in the midst, and above all, the crucified and exalted one, exposing this world's evil, and fulfilling his own prophecy and promise. 'Now is the judgment of this world; now shall the ruler of this world be cast out; and I, when I am lifted up from the earth, will draw all men to myself.' (John 12:32). Therefore in this incident we find ourselves beginning to be faced acutely by the same deep and perplexing issues of human life, sin and suffering that are now settled for ever by what happened in the Cross. It may be that we are meant already to see in Solomon, a foreshadowing of him who was 'greater than Solomon.' (Matt. 12:42).

Points for Further Thought and Discussion

In the Old Testament such vivid experiences as this dream-vision were often regarded by those who received them, as significant and helpful at the beginning of their service of God. Are we to expect such in our New Testament experience?

What place should 'asking' take in our prayer life today? What does the New Testament suggest? Discuss the text 'You do not have because you do not ask' (James 4:2) in its relevance to ourselves, our Church and our nation.

Are our priorities in life still revealed to God in what we pray for? Are we, too, tested and judged on this point? What should our priorities be for ourselves in our own praying within the world today?

Note how confident God was in the kind of king Solomon would become. Later on, as we already know, he greatly fell short of the ideal. Are we to admit that God was mistaken or surprised – and does he still remain all-knowing and all-powerful? What are we to think? What does the Bible say?

Can you think of spheres of public life, and aspects of our own life in which we cannot hope to make wise judgements except through prayer and its answer?

Can you think of situations in which living very near to genuine goodness actually provokes anger, and even hatred, on the part of those who do not have any love for it. Might this be a factor in explaining why Jesus was crucified and why he said 'Now is the judgement of this world'?

Notes

Low estimates of Solomon
'The reign of Solomon', says Adam Clarke, the famous eighteenth century Methodist commentator, 'began inauspiciously: even a brother's blood must be shed to cause

him to sit securely on his throne, and a most reprehensible alliance, the forerunner of many others, was formed for the same purpose. Solomon had many advantages and no man ever made worse use of them'. Such commentators interpret Solomon's 'love for the Lord,' as being a purely formal affair – lavish and expensive observance of sacrifice without the heart's devotion! We believe that such comment at this stage in his life is unjustifiable.

Solomon's dream–encounter with God

It was acknowledged within Israel that God could communicate his will to his people through dreams, visions and through the word of prophets (cf. 1 Sam. 28:6,15; Joel 2:28) and even in New Testament times his use of dreams and 'visions in the night' continued (Matt. 1:20; Acts 10:3; 16:9). There is, however, something quite unique about Solomon's experience in this case. Though when he woke up he knew he had been in a dream-state, he had no doubt that in what happened in the dream there had taken place a decisive personal encounter with God, that he himself had made a solemn life-commitment, and that promises had been made to him that were to affect the future of Israel and his whole personal career. It is noteworthy that the two recorded communications between God and Solomon take place not, as usual with the kings of Israel, through prophet or priest, but through dreams in a sacred place.

Stories of 'wise' judgements

As examples of stories similar to that of Solomon, there has been cited that of the king of Thrace who decided who was genuine among three claimants to be heirs of a dead king, by ordering them to pierce the corpse of the father with a spear, thus singling out the genuine son by his refusal to obey. There is also the Indian story of a goddess who reveals the genuine mother of a child by a command to seize its arms and legs, and pull it apart.

CHAPTER IV

SOLOMON AND THE BUILDING OF THE TEMPLE
I Kings 4: 1 – 6:14

The Narrative

We are given here a brief account of the wisdom, wealth, and fame that immediately marked Solomon's reign. Yet from its beginning he remembered the vow given to his father and was possessed by one divinely inspired aim – to build the temple. In this accomplishment we are shown how his insight, influence with Hiram, organising ability and wisdom all play their part. Yet it is God's inspiration and providential control that bring success.

Wisdom, Wealth and Fame

Though Solomon's early reign is described here only in a series of historical news items and sketchy reports, we are meant to be impressed by how soon and fully God fulfilled his promise, 'there will never have been anyone like you, nor will there ever be.' (N.I.V.3:12) When he came to his throne there was peace in all the surrounding areas. Moreover those nations from whom his father, David, exacted tribute continued faithfully to pay their dues so that wealth flowed into the land of Israel (4:24). The writer of this account, who may be looking back from a much later time, tells us that the whole nation then actually enjoyed the conditions dreamed of by patriarchs and prophets as belonging to the future kingdom of the Messiah: '*Judah and Israel were as many as the sand by the seashore*' (cf. Gen. 22:7) and each lived in safety and happiness '*under his own vine and fig tree*' (4:25, cf. Mic. 4:4; Zech. 3:10).

Though all this is to be understood as the providential work
of God, Solomon himself is to be given credit for several
important features of this period of his reign. The account
indicates the efficiency of his administration. For his central
government he tried to find from around him trustworthy
people with special ability for particular jobs, (4:1–4). For local
affairs, he ignored the exact tribal boundaries which hindered
progress, and divided the country into what he felt to be
manageable areas under reliable appointees (4:7–19).

It was no doubt through such wise administration that at
this stage of his life he was able to allow all his subjects some
share in the prosperity of the whole community. In every
affluent society there is always a tendency for wealth to flow to
those who have it, so that rich and powerful become more
rich, and the poor and weak become more poor. Towards the
end of his reign Solomon grew careless, and having lost his
early ideals had to face much bitterness amongst the deprived
in his community, but here in his early years he was more
careful.

Thankfully he was able to moderate the flow of wealth into
his own coffers. Only for one month in twelve was each region
burdened with meeting its share in the upkeep of his court
and central administration. A nineteenth century
commentator notes that whereas the splendour of the royal
households in his own day in Europe was often the sign of the
oppression of the people, here in the case of Solomon it showed
their happiness and prosperity!

Solomon made a very wide use of the divinely given insight
into human affairs which had already brought him fame as a
judge. Everywhere in the Middle East even in those days the
advice of 'wise men' (and women, too) was sought after by
the common people who wanted counselling, and in the
important centres of government there were often schools of
wisdom where people could receive advice to help them live
successfully, to cope adequately with life's many problems, and
reflect on the meaning and purpose of life. This wisdom was
often communicated in the form of proverbs, sayings put in
concise and memorable form. Solomon composed such words.
He also wrote lyrics in poetical form put to music. No doubt in
Solomon's case his 'wisdom' reflected his understanding of

God's ways. (4:29–34).

The gift of wisdom seems to have given him a unique sensitivity towards the creatures God had put in the world around him. He was a keen observer of the way plants grow, and of the habits and instincts of animals, and in his proverbs he was able to draw lessons from such aspects of life around him to illustrate his wise teachings. He was conscious that the redeeming God of Israel, the God of Abraham and of David, was the one whose creative love lay behind everything he had brought into existence on this earth. Such appreciation, love and respect for the natural world around us reflects the sympathetic insight which God gave to Adam when he gave each kind of animal the name he considered to suit it (Gen. 2:19–20), and, of course, made him a loving gardener (Gen. 2:15). In our modern 'green' and ecology movements it is a good sign that we are conscious of our need to recover this 'wisdom' of Solomon even while we 'have dominion over the earth' (Gen. 1:28).

A Temple 'for the Name of the Lord'

In contrast to the concise brevity of the fourth chapter which we have just surveyed, the following three lengthy chapters go into much detail in their description of Solomon's greatest work. In the midst of all the fame and wealth with which he soon found himself surrounded, he never for one moment allowed himself to forget that he had been raised up by God for one supreme purpose – to build the temple. For him at this stage of his life no other achievement would have been worth while had this not been accomplished.

Early in his reign he felt himself challenged to begin. In the peace he enjoyed he saw simply an opportunity opened up by God for this particular work. His wealth was simply God's provision for its accomplishment. What he lacked were the skills and materials needed for such a vast enterprise, and when King Hiram of Tyre, attracted by his growing fame, made a friendly and admiring approach to him, he immediately recognised this too as a divinely given opportunity. Hiram had at his disposal everything that in any way was required, and there was no need for delay in going ahead. Hiram, too, had been a friend and admirer of David's and was in a position to understand his aims and motives. In the letter to Hiram, his hoped-for ally, begging his practical help, he tried to explain the unfulfilled urge and disappointment of his father in not being able to complete his life's work and the vision that he himself now shared of a temple '*for the name of the Lord*' (5:5).

This arresting phrase can introduce us at this point to one of the aims he and his father sought so earnestly to achieve in the building of this temple. When Moses at the burning bush asked God his name, he was given an answer that, however we interpret it, must have seemed at the time difficult to understand. 'I am that I am', God said. Some scholars think that this is better translated as 'I will be whom I will be'. God here seems to be telling Moses that only time and history will spell out who he is, and what his name will be. He also told Moses there and then that he was the God who had already made his name known in the history of Abraham, Isaac and Jacob, 'the Lord, the God of your fathers' (cf. Exod. 3:13–15). Both David and Solomon in their day knew and understood much more about the name of God than Moses did at the burning bush. For them history had already spelt out his wonderful name in the deliverance of his people from Egypt, in the revelation of the law given at Sinai, in all the great things that had proved his faithfulness and love for his people during the wilderness wanderings and the conquest of Canaan, and in events such as the slaying of Goliath. No other God had such a glorious 'name' which must be commemorated and published for ages to come. No other nation had a God so good and true! But all the other nations had at the centre of their life impressive temples for their idols so that their people could see and worship them. Now that Israel had settled, and the days of their wanderings were over, it had come to both David and Solomon with an overwhelming conviction that the Lord desired there in Jerusalem a temple 'for his name' It was to be not a centre for the adoration of an idol or an image but a place towards which all his people could turn and look from anywhere when they needed help, a house in which they could

gather with their joyfully offered sacrifices, to be reminded of
the glory of his name through proclamation and liturgy and
seek his blessing and peace and salvation (see note).

When everything was ready, and enough materials were
assembled at the site, Solomon chose for the time when the
work was to begin, a significant date, marked as exactly as
possible twelve generations (480 years) from the time that Israel
experienced its marvellous deliverance at the Red Sea. In
Solomon's mind the building of this temple was now to mark
the beginning of a new era in the life of God's people (6:1).

Solomon Builds – with God

The description of the work, men and materials involved (5:13–
17), brings before us the vastness and complicated nature of
the task – thirty thousand labourers, seventy thousand carriers,
eighty thousand stone cutters, and 3300 foremen. Whereas he
appointed a team to help him to govern the country, the
indication is that Solomon supervised and managed all this by
himself, giving even express personal instructions that the stone
cutting should be done as he wanted (5:17). We are told too
that he personally saw to it that the payments of wheat, and
olive oil, were regularly made from his side to keep the work
going on Hiram's side (5:10–11).

One feature of the management is extremely important.
Solomon laid down and demanded exactness in all the details
of the work. No sloppiness could be tolerated. The standard
was perfection, and each part must meet that standard before
it was sent to Jerusalem. *'Neither hammer, nor axe, nor any tool of
iron was heard in the temple while it was being built'* (6:7).
Commentators have speculated to find some allegorical
meaning for this requirement 'The temple' says one, 'was a
type of the kingdom of God. The souls of men are to be fully
prepared *here* for that place of blessedness – no preachings or
exhortations or tears or cries up there to fit us for a place in
the New Jerusalem'! Another comments: 'Noise in Lebanon,
nothing in Sion, but silence and peace. O God that the axes of
schism, or the hammers of factious contentions should be
heard in thy sanctuary!' Perhaps Solomon simply wanted to

make it clear to everyone concerned and everyone who witnessed its marvellous construction that here in this building was a unique event in the history of the world. Where in history had their ever been set such a standard? Where in history had there ever been such a building?

It took seven years to build the temple. The difficulties were enormous and human morale must have tended at times to flag. It was no doubt at a point in the middle of some of these discouragements, when he needed strength, that '*the word of the Lord came to Solomon*' (6:11–14) with the promise of final success as the reward for faithfulness. It is immediately after this word that we have the verse: '*So Solomon built the temple and completed it.*' The temple was built because God himself was always there in the midst with his word inspiring and controlling the project, and finally bringing it to completion.

We are explicitly told at one point that the peaceful relations between Hiram and Solomon which so miraculously prevailed during the period of the building were sustained because '*the Lord gave Solomon wisdom.*' We have to give God the credit, too, for the fact that Solomon found around him so much willing co-operation from masses of people who seemed to share his vision and hope. 'Your troops shall be willing on your day of battle' (Ps.110:3 N.I.V.) was one of the promises on which a king in Israel was meant to rely. The reader of the narrative can be taken back in memory to what happened when Moses was making the tabernacle in the wilderness. He found around him not only enough skilled persons to whom the Lord had given ability, but also an extraordinary spirit of co-operation and unity among his people. They brought 'much more than enough' to do all the work, and had to be restrained from doing more (Exod. 36: 5–6).

A Fault -Overlooked!

Before we move on, there is one aspect of the building of the temple which we have to question. Why did Solomon resort to '*forced labour*' (5:13–14)? Why, in the midst of so much dedicated effort to glorify God and advance his kingdom did he fail at this one point to continue to trust in the influence of the Spirit of God, and in God's promise to honour those who trusted in him alone? God, he knew, was a God of freely given love, who sought from those who called on his name only the freely given response of heart and mind. We can understand conscription for an army in a national emergency, but God could not have meant his temple to be built by any form of slavery. It was an extraordinary lapse that, facing this important issue, he should have allowed himself to be prompted solely by his own purely human wisdom and to become dependent on his own kingly power, and the ways of this world. It was, however, an early sign of a blind spot in his vision of God and the purpose for which he had been called to live his whole life. Had his heart and mind been wholly devoted to God he would have recognised that by choosing such means to further his achievement he was putting out a false message about God's ways, both to his own people and to the surrounding nations.

God certainly overlooked this fault there and then, and the reference to it in this passage can be read as if it were merely a passing incident. Solomon is soon to be lavishly praised for what he has accomplished. We ourselves can take comfort in the fact that God does not always and immediately mark iniquity, and reject imperfect work. Even in our own most wholehearted attempts to please him, he has time and again to ignore the faults which, if taken into account, could make them worthless. 'Like a father', says Calvin, 'God is pleased to watch and accept our efforts, as those of a little child, even though they are worth nothing.' We each have to learn that we need to have not only our persons forgiven by God, but also even our best works.

Though overlooked by God within the affairs of the moment, however, the fault is clearly mentioned. The writer of the history obviously intends us to notice how badly it spoils his otherwise noble picture of Solomon. The notice of it brings before us a question often raised in Holy Scripture: Where have we to fix our trust as we seek to spread the good news of the Gospel, build the Church, and advance the kingdom of God? When the temple was being rebuilt, the prophet Zechariah reminded Zerubbabel and his colleagues that God willed the work to be accomplished,' not by might, nor by power, but by my Spirit' (Zech. 4:6). How easy it is for us to lapse! For instance in our efforts to teach and preach in Christ's name are we not prone at times to trust in our own eloquence, or scholarship, or our theological insight rather than the power of the Spirit of God.? And in our attempts at church building do we not at times distort the pastoral image which God means to shine through its fellowship, by resorting to the ways of the world in pushing things on and getting things done with technological and bureaucratic efficiency? How differently it all happened on the first Palm Sunday when the King of Kings gave us a glimpse of the way he meant us to take, by choosing the way towards his own throne and reign, seeking the alliance only of those drawn by his personal worth.

Points for Further Thought and Discussion

Was it especially difficult for Solomon in the midst of his wealth to please God? Does wealth hinder us ourselves, or church, or nation from pleasing God?

Is this example of God's making his people depend on help from the heathen for furthering his work an illustration of how we, in the Church today should be willing at times to accept outside help?

In the light of what is said about Solomon's sensitivity to the natural world, discuss this verse of a well known hymn:
    'Heaven above is softer blue,
    Earth around is sweeter green;
    Something lives in every hue,
    Christless eyes have never seen.'

Solomon was inspired to build the temple not only by a vision of what it could stand for in Israel's religious life, but also by a vow by which his father had pledged him. Discuss the place that can be taken by fulfilling solemn public vows in living our Christian lives, and in the service of the Church.

Discuss how, in some of the important tasks God gives us to do within the Church, we tend to put our trust in the effectiveness of our purely human gifts and methods, rather than in the living power of the Spirit of God, and sometimes resort to unworthy ways and means.

Notes

The 'wisdom of Solomon'
At the time of Solomon the nations and empires surrounding Israel had each also their store of wisdom literature such as we have in the Bible. It took various forms – proverbs, poems, dramas, riddles etc. and formed the basis of the contemporary educational system in schools of wisdom which flourished especially among the aristocratic classes. Such wisdom gave

expression to what people had found in their culture to be the best way to react to life's problems, to overcome trauma, to be successful in business and court life. It taught what builds up community life and leads to human happiness and general well-being. It was taught by acknowledged teachers. It had been described as 'the earliest form of scientific understanding of life' describing a rule of life for those who accepted its discipline. (Von Rad)

It was this same kind of wisdom which then flourished in Israel under the leadership of Solomon. It produced 'wise men' (cf. Jer. 8:4; 9:23 and women too e.g. 2 Sam. 14:2–4). Much of Israel's wisdom was similar in form and content to that of other nations but it took account of the fact that 'the fear of the Lord is the beginning of wisdom' (Prov. 1:7), and that life must be lived under his eye and in his service. It is when we come to our discussion of chapter 10 that we will be shown the superiority of Solomon's wisdom to that of all other nations.

The Temple and the Name of the Lord

It becomes clear that, though Solomon had it in mind to build a house worthy of the honour due to him among nations, one of his chief purposes was that there should be a final and settled place where his 'name' could be called upon by his people for ever as they expressed their devotion and sought his help. Abraham had had chosen altars in Canaan where God appeared and he did this (Gen. 12:8; cf. 13:14). The promise had been given: 'In every place where I cause my name to be remembered, I will come to you and bless you' (Exod. 20:24). But now, as God had chosen David, given him the Holy City and called for the temple to be built, the conviction began to grow that God had chosen that his name should be associated finally with this place. It was of this temple that he said, 'My name shall be there' (Deut. 12:15,11; 14:23–24; 16:2,6,11; 26:2). The temple was now to be the place where it was certain, God would hear prayer. It will become clear as we go through Solomon's words in chapter 8, that prayer from any location, even from another land, would now become effective if it was directed towards this temple (1 Kings 8:42,48). Jeroboam's chief sin was to prevent his people from even directing their prayer and worship towards this sanctuary (1 Kings 12:27). When the book of Deuteronomy was re-discovered and read to King Josiah it was interpreted as forbidding the worship of the Lord in any other centre than at Jerusalem (2 Kings: 23:8–12).

CHAPTER V

THE HOLY PLACE, THE TEMPLE-SURROUNDINGS AND FURNISHING.

I Kings 6: 15 – 7:51

The Narrative

This passage, dealing with various aspects of the design of the temple, brings before us three different matters, all of interest and of varied importance. Our thoughts are first drawn to the inner sanctuary, the place of the ark at the heart of the temple, then to the massive complex of public buildings very near to it, then to the beauty and costliness of the internal furnishings made for use within its courts.

The Heart of the Temple

Our attention first becomes focused on the construction of *'an inner sanctuary ... the most holy place'* (6:16). It was to be the central feature of the whole building – a place set apart at its rear, square in its dimensions, and curtained off by delicately carved doors. Its dark interior was dominated by two great cherubim, each the height of the whole structure, made of olive wood covered with gold. The extended wings of each touched in the centre and reached each side wall. Between and under these cherubim was the place where the ark of God was finally to be placed.

While the Israelites were still around Sinai in the wilderness, God had ordered the making of the ark to contain the two tablets of stone. It had been put within the tabernacle in the wilderness, and when Moses presented himself he found God again present to meet and speak with him as he had done on

43

the holy mountain. The ark was given by God to Israel to be the sign of his presence. It was sometimes taken into their midst as they entered battle. It was carried before them on their travels. When they reached the Jordan, ready to enter the promised land, the priests were ordered to carry the ark into the river, and the waters divided and retreated on each side so that the people could go over on dry land. It had been from the ark in the tabernacle that the word of the Lord had first come to Samuel. It had suffered abuse and had been miraculously rescued by God. It had been neglected and laid aside. Yet it had been marvellously preserved as if for the new future that lay before God's people during their settled residence in the promised land.

David had been possessed by a longing, which he believed was from God, to bring the ark back to the centre of Israel's life, and one of his chief aims in his desire to build the temple was that it should have at its centre a fitting place in which the ark could rest. Here in the temple it was to be a sign of God's presence, faithfulness, mercy and power. Towards it his people would look as they brought their sacrifices, sought to see the gracious face of the Lord, to hear his word and have the assurance that they were accepted in love as his people. But here also it was to be placed to remind them of God's holiness and justice and to inspire them with the same awe and fear as had made Moses at times hide his face in approaching God. This was why it was to be lodged, hidden in apartness, in the midst of mystery and darkness. Only the high priest dared enter that inner sanctuary, only once a year, and that when the blood of atonement had been shed for all that most deeply troubled the human conscience.

Therefore here in the place that might be occupied in the temple of other nations by a great altar for sacrifice to appease their God, or by an impressive image to evoke exciting religious response, there was this strange inner temple reminding them that the Lord, the God of Israel was the 'same yesterday, today, and for ever'. They were to be always his people, and he would be ever their God, the Holy One of Israel.

God's presence in forgiving love and in holy apartness! They could find him, trust him, and rejoice in his true light even though his ways were beyond all understanding!

The Setting of the Temple

As we read on we are suddenly told that, as well as spending seven years on the temple, Solomon spent thirteen years on the construction of his own palace, built it next door to the temple and filled the whole area around with an array of large government halls as splendidly constructed as the temple itself, including a palace for Pharoah's daughter whom he had married. Including the temple, six buildings are mentioned. They were all built on one site and enclosed together by one outer wall, though the temple stood at the north end of the whole complex on a slightly higher level within a court cordoned off by its own wall. The buildings are mentioned in the text as one would enter them from the southern end of the site. The first, described in some detail, was the '*House of the Forest of Lebanon*' (7:2). It was given its name because the number and siting of its cedar pillars gave it such an inside appearance. It was larger than the temple, suitable for large gatherings and also served as a place for the display of specially precious objects of public interest (cf. 10:16–17). The next building on the list is the '*Hall of Pillars*' (7:6) which seems to have been a waiting room or entrance hall for access to the '*Hall of the Throne*' (7:7) – the place where the king could be met, sitting on his throne to rule in justice and give decisions in matters of state. The king was himself given easy access to the Throne Hall from the immediately adjacent Royal Palace –'*his own house where he was to dwell*' (7:8), and in an adjacent palace he housed the daughter of Pharoah, his queen. Solomon saw to it that from his palace he had easy access not only to his Throne Hall but also to the temple itself through a convenient door in the outer wall. It is mentioned in the text that the stones of the public buildings were made from the soft limestone of the district, which before it had hardened by being exposed to the air, could be shaped with the saw (7:9–12).

Though in his design and the construction of the inside of the temple, Solomon was so careful to give a clear witness to the apartness and holiness of God, he nevertheless ensured that its site at the heart of the community should bear witness to a God who also desired to be near to his people, and indeed, involved in all their important social and political affairs.

We are justified in assuming that the relative siting of the temple alongside the royal residence and these halls of government and justice, was as deliberately planned by Solomon as was its internal architecture. The young king at this stage in his career shared something of his father's vision of Jerusalem as the city of God and he was likely to have regarded all these buildings for 'public' administration as built for, and dedicated to, the service of the one God who was to be met and worshipped in his sanctuary. After all, for him the 'fear of the Lord' was the 'beginning of wisdom', and the ark itself contained the tablets of the law.

It was Solomon's plan also to have the temple placed where he could conveniently watch over it. It was a tradition he had inherited. Moses, the greatest leader ever of his nation, had directed and controlled every aspect of its religious life. David, his father, had followed this example. He himself at this time in his life was convinced that he was called by God to maintain the temple he had built and to guide all its affairs. We cannot blame him for having this concern. We will discover as we read through the Book of Kings that those rulers such as Hezekiah and Josiah who most pleased God were those who kept in mind this pattern of kingship over every aspect of the nation's life (see note).

Worthiness and Worship

After his comparatively brief account of Solomon's work on the great surrounding buildings, the writer suddenly returns to a description of the intense care and thought he put into the completion of his work on the temple itself. We have here almost a whole chapter devoted to the listing, designing, specification, ordering and manufacture of all the furnishings and utensils that were finally to be required before the temple could be dedicated and put to use. Everything for constant public exposure and use had to be bronze, a metal with a strong enduring quality which could be burnished to have its own unique splendour. Though Solomon, later, dazzled the whole world around him with the splendour of his earthly throne, and though he had to spend more time on the construction of government buildings and palaces than the seven years he

spent on the temple, there is no suggestion that the treasures
he made for God's house were of secondary concern.

No one in Israel had the craftsmanship required. The finest
artist in the whole world was chosen even though he was trained
abroad and had some heathen kinship. A special foundry for
his work was set up in the plain of the Jordan. In what was offered
and set to use before God in the temple no cost was spared.
Infinite care and consideration given to every detail. Nothing
was second rate. Solomon obviously believed that everything
within the temple should speak not only of God's faithfulness
and majesty but also enable his people to worship in a response
that reflected an appreciation of the costliness of his love.

There was much that was pleasing to the eye, as well as useful.
We are given elaborate details of two bronze pillars, one called
'Jachin' and the other 'Boaz' which were placed in the
vestibule. They did not support the roof but were largely
ornamental (7:15–22). A prominent object at the south-east
corner of the temple area was a huge basin of bronze supported
by twelve statues of bulls in groups of three facing outwards.
Filled with water it was able to hold 10,000 gallons. As an
example of skill in bronze construction and of the craftsman's
art it was a masterpiece. It was used by the priests to replenish
their own utensils with water when it was needed, and it may
also at one time have had a symbolic meaning (7:23–26). There
were ten mobile stands each with four wheels and holding 200
gallons. These too were of elaborate construction and richly
decorated. They stood normally in rows, five on the left side
and five on the right side of the temple, and were used for
washing the sacrifices (7:27–39). It is repeated, as if were
important, that the very pots for cooking the shared sacrificial
meals and the shovels for collecting the ashes of the fires were
made for king Solomon with no less care, by Hiram too, and
were of the same burnished bronze (7: 40–50). Even gold was
lavishly used here and there for more delicate objects such as
tables of incense and candlesticks – and amazingly, for the
hinges of some doors (7:48–50). In addition there were
deposited among the sacred objects all treasures which David
had collected and handed down for the temple use.

Of course we have to learn from the New Testament what
pleases God most in the way we worship him. Jesus taught us

that God seeks and finds the true worship which pleases him in the spontaneous total and loving response which the Holy Spirit inspires when his truth is revealed and proclaimed to us. He rejoiced when he found such worship given to him by the woman at the well, (John 4: 23–24)) and by the blind man whose eyes he had formerly restored (John 9:38). His praise when he saw the widow offering her mite (Luke 21:3) reminds us that the worth of what we offer does not lie in its commercial or intrinsic value, but in what it costs the worshipper who makes the offering.

It will become obvious as we read through the next chapter in our account of his life that Solomon was aware of what lay at the essential heart of true worship. He did not imagine that God's own glory could be represented by the work of human artists or the great buildings which we can produce to the glory of his name. No other image of God must be set up along side the mystery of holiness, love, and majesty represented by the ark there in the holy of holies! He well knew that if ever true worship was to take place in his newly built temple then God must himself come into the midst, give himself to be worshipped in his gracious and pardoning presence to those who come seeking him with contrite and believing hearts. He knew well that God loved to be worshipped in the 'splendour of holiness' rather than in the splendour of the great building and its elaborate and even costly embellishments. But he did believe that in our worshipful response and its accompaniments nothing should be cheap or unworthy of the name of the Lord. He had no doubt learned how his father David on an important occasion in his life had said, 'I will not sacrifice to the Lord burnt offerings that cost me nothing' (2 Sam. 24:24)

We must be continually asking ourselves about the quality of what we are offering to God when we respond to his grace in worship. Is it worthy? Does it match the resources at our disposal, and our expenditure in the secular world? Are we giving him the very best? This can refer to everything we can create or devise or use or purchase or build or hire to the glory of his name. It can refer to the kind of music we indulge in. It can refer to the effort and study we put into the preparation of what is to be said and done at a worship service. It can refer even to our dress and the attitude and posture we adopt within the gathered congregation. Is it not a healthy instinct to be ashamed of what we are offering if it costs us nothing to give it, and our attitude is careless and casual?

The Glory in the midst of the Vanity

Solomon, undoubtedly, in his efforts to build the temple, had the glory of God in mind. He prayed and God answered him. What he did was accepted by God as a significant and hopeful development in the earthly history of the people of God.

Yet even as we read about his remarkable achievement, we are made aware of a persistent flaw in his reponse to the grace of God – a flaw that threatens to spoil what God is seeking to do with him and through him. His later history will bring it out more clearly but it is already noticeable. He is prone to seek personal grandeur and in pursuit of it is becoming dominated by a passion to build in stone and lime and cedar. These faults will ultimately distance him from a large and deprived section of his people, lead to their neglect, and finally to a tragic split in his kingdom.

Moreover, we are soon to discover, as we read through the ensuing story, that the central feature in the very set-up in the temple area – the close togetherness which he established between his royal buildings, his own house, and the House of God – served in the long run rather to defile the temple than to sanctify his civil government (see note). The subsequent history will show us that his zeal to build became a personal passion that led him to neglect the welfare of an important section of his people and led to his kingdom being split in two. The temple itself proved soon to have too many costly treasures where thieves could break in and steal. Its wealth was soon plundered both by foreign invaders and by its own royal custodians. Several of its kings even perverted its worship and set up pagan altars within it, encouraged only those priests who allowed them their own way, and persecuted the prophets whom God sent to correct them. Finally Solomon's 'temple for the name of the Lord', instead of a renewing influence in the social life of the nation, became the centre of a false and vicious religion.

We will have to face all these matters squarely as the history unfolds. The writer, at present, however means us to appreciate all the more fully the marvellous way in which God holds firmly on to this frail man and continues to work with him and through him. The next three chapters of the book are there to show us that, in spite of these threatening defects, God was continuing to work powerfully through what Solomon was seeking to achieve, and to fulfil his early promise of greatness in wisdom and wealth. God was there crowning his efforts with success and bringing his inspired hopes to fruition. The eighth chapter which we are about to read, will show how he sealed with his gracious presence the dedication of the temple buildings, and gave such signs of his approval of its ritual and worship that even after its destruction his successors felt they had to rebuild as he had done. The following two chapters will show how God accepted his efforts to become a good and wise king, overruling the undesirable aspects of his rule, and creating through him a model and pattern of kingly greatness from which we ourselves are meant to learn something of the ways and purposes of God in human history and in which we can find a significant pattern of the glory of the coming Messiah. Certainly in the course of this development Solomon had to be kept on his course by severe warning, but the purpose of the warning was simply that God's great work with him might be all the more fully accomplished.

There is much that is depressing to the reader in the Book of Kings – the story of the decline and fall of the monarchy in Israel. We are meant, however, to take heart in these signs that will be given to us, time and again, here and there, that where sin begins to reign, God makes his grace all the more abound (Rom. 5:20). It is important that as we read through this book we should notice not only the vanity in the midst of the glory, but also the glory in the midst of the vanity. God, even today, whenever he can find the faith and submission of a human mind and will, however weak, can go to work powerfully in the midst of all the surrounding decadence,and give us marvellous signs of his power to renew his creation and bring about the fulfilment of his promises.

Points for Further Thought and Discussion

David and Solomon believed that God would make himself present in the midst of his worshippers and followers where the ark was honoured, and his love and faithfulness were remembered. Through what means and under what conditions are we to expect to find his presence in our midst to be encountered in worship today?

Should the Church of today expect or claim more encouragement or privileges from its civil government than the freedom to worship, propagate its teachings and train its young?

Think over the following incidents and texts : Luke 10: 39–42, Mark 14:3 – 9, Luke 5:8 What do they tell us about what Jesus seeks from us in our worship?

In what ways are we ourselves, in our particular circumstances today, tempted to respond unworthily to the costly revelation of God's love in Christ? – in matters of Church worship and witness, by being, for example, slovenly, ill prepared, cheap or self centred.

Think of ways in which the circumstances in which we ourselves live and work today show a similarity with those which prevailed under Solomon in the Book of Kings. In what features of God's work and power can we take courage and comfort today?

Note

Ezekiel's ideal vision.
In exile in Babylon, God gave Ezekiel a vision of a new temple built no longer close to, but in isolation from, those who were to have rule over civil affairs. 'The house of Israel', he said, 'will never again defile my holy name – neither they nor their kings – by their prostitution... when they placed their threshold next to my threshold and their doorposts beside my doorposts; with only a wall between me and them' (Ezek. 43:1–12, N.I.V.). But now, free and cleansed from such close defilement, a

wonderful transformation was to occur. The new and isolated temple was to become the source of a stream of living and refreshing waters bringing new life and social health to the very world from which it had been set apart by God (Ezek. 47:1–12).

We are not meant to dismiss entirely Solomon's vision of a temple at the heart of a nation's life, but we must not forget the warning of Ezekiel and lose our vision, our power and our message by being too open to the world we are meant to save.

PLAN OF TEMPLE

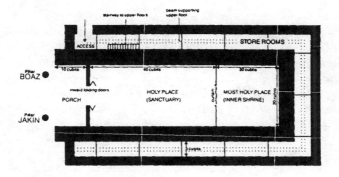

Adjacent Administrative Buildings
(on a much smaller scale. The temple itself was smaller than
the 'House of Lebanon')

TEMPLE AREA

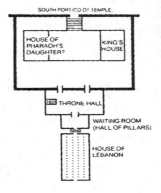

Chapter VI

THE LORD COMES TO HIS TEMPLE
1 Kings 8: 1–66

The Narrative

At the dedication of the finished temple building, the
ark was solemnly placed in its inner sanctuary. As the
priests withdrew, they themselves, and the congregation,
were overwhelmed by the descent of the same kind of
cloud as had been the sign of God's presence in the
wilderness. Solomon in an utterance of praise,
intercession and dedication, assumed the leadership of
the whole service, expressed his wonder at the mystery of
God's presence with man, and led his people in a
memorable prayer.

The Great Moment

The whole nation gathered for celebration when the
temple was dedicated during the feast of Tabernacles at
Jerusalem. They sacrificed '*so many sheep and cattle that they
could not be counted*' (v.5). But everything finally centred
on the ark, and the great moment to which everyone
looked forward was when it was finally laid by the priests
in the place that had been made for it in the inner
sanctuary. We can imagine what they felt, and what their
prayers were.

They were of course pledging their loyalty. The very act of
placing the ark where it was in future to rest was a sign to God
that they wanted to keep always at the heart of their religious
life everything this ark had stood for, and had given to their

54

fathers. It was a plea to God to be their inspiration, guardian and guide from now on with the same care as he had shown to them in the wilderness. It was a promise that they would continue to be his covenant people and to keep his commandments.

They were also invoking God's presence. They had constructed the temple, with its outer sanctuary and its inner 'holy of holies' to correspond to the design given by God himself to Moses for the tabernacle in the wilderness. God had honoured Moses' efforts to follow this heavenly pattern, and in the wilderness tabernacle had made his presence known continually. Undoubtedly Solomon and his people hoped and prayed that God would do for them and their children after them in this great sanctuary no less than he had done for Moses and his people. As we read through the account of how they brought up the ark to its new dwelling place, we are reminded of the central verses of one of the Psalms written to be sung to God himself as an invitation to enter through doors specially opened for him.

> Lift up your heads, O gates!
> and be lifted up, O ancient doors!
> that the King of glory may come in.
> Who is the King of glory?
> The Lord of hosts
> he is the King of glory! (Ps. 24:7–10)

Not long after the capture of Jerusalem by David, the ark was solemnly and joyfully brought up to the hill of Zion and through the 'ancient gates' of the holy city to be installed in the temporary tabernacle that had been created for it. It is probable that this psalm was originally written on this occasion. Solomon remembered that his father had regarded the entry of the ark into his city as the entry of the Lord himself to reign there, and David's great hymn was sung again with hope and prayers, as the ark entered the place now designed to represent the earthly throne of God.

The answer to their trembling hope was an event that surpassed their greatest expectation. It reminded them of the

great moment in past history when God was calling them to
launch out on their long and hard journey through the
wilderness from Sinai. As a pledge that he would be with
them 'the cloud covered the tent of meeting and the glory
of the Lord filled the tabernacle' (Exod. 40:34–5).
Suddenly, again, the same kind of cloud with the brightness
of God's glory, but with great darkness at its heart
descended to fill the inner shrine. God himself was there!
There was no noise. Not even a voice from heaven. Nothing
needed to be said. Immediately all who were there saw it
as marvellous and understood what it meant. It was a sign
of God's acknowledgement of this place as his chosen
dwelling place on earth. He had been there guiding their
father David when he bought the site. He had been there
directing the minds of those who had planned its
construction. It was not they who had set it up for him but
he who had chosen it for himself. It was a pledge about
their whole future. Here was, from now on, the appointed
place where God would certainly be sought and found.
Here sinners would find atonement, forgiveness and new
life. Here his face would be seen by those who had been in
darkness and sought light. Here his word would be heard.

Solomon before God and his People

The coming of the cloud was, of course, God's crowning
acknowledgement of the plans, prayers and dreams of David
and Solomon himself, and it was Solomon's greatest hour. The
priests were overwhelmed. Their planned ritual was cut short.
It was the king's moment and he took the lead.

It is obvious that at this point in his career he had already
the respect and trust of his own people. He could summon
them into his presence (v. 1) and *they assembled to him* (v. 5)
And now at the height of their celebration they listened to
him as ardently as their forefathers had listened to Moses and
Joshua. Here was a king who knew God, who had his favour,
and was like a father to his people. All the words he said were
remembered and recorded as '*he stood and blessed all the assembly
of Israel with a loud voice*' (v. 55) exhorting them as a prophet

and priest. When the time of sacrifice came it was he who made the offerings. When he sent them away *'they blessed the king and went to their homes joyful and glad of heart'* (v. 66).

God not only honoured Solomon before his people, he also inspired him to give one of the most memorable of all the occasional utterances that we can find in the pages of the Old Testament. It was certainly for him a time of deep religious emotion. He was exultant and uplifted in heart as he spoke. Other men of God would have expressed their intimate personal feelings more unrestrainedly. We can remember David dancing before the Lord on an occasion quite similar to this. Solomon was not that type. His was always a controlled and even dignified type of piety, which never indulges in any kind of charismatic outburst, but which is as completely genuine as that which does. Therefore in his address to God he uses what seems to us the formal language of a regular church liturgy. This must not, however, conceal from us the deeply felt fervour and joy that for him marked the whole happening. In the autobiography of C. F. Andrews who was a prominent missionary to India early this century, we have an account of how, on the morning after his deep conversion experience, he attended a little Anglican Church in the country, and of how the routine words of the liturgy and benediction took life, and brought 'wave upon wave' of blessing. So it must have been with Solomon that day. Here we have a man pouring out his heart before God with a note of urgent personal intensity. As he leads the community in prayer, they sense that he is really praying as they join with him. And they can join with him because his prayer is made up of commonly known expressions and uttered with complete simplicity.

He expressed his wonder at the miracle of divine condescension. What had happened was impossible *'Behold, the heaven and the highest heaven cannot contain thee. How much less this house which I have built!'* (v. 27) – and yet it had happened!

Moreover he expressed his deep perplexity at the miracle of divine self-revelation. The cloud which had been so radiant with the light of the glory of the God of Israel had also enveloped within itself a deep darkness! – God was the one whose nature and ways had to be acknowledged as beyond

human comprehension and yet he had come into their midst
and again proved he had a heart of mercy. He had set up a
dwelling place for himself on earth so that he could be helpful!
He had even used Solomon to build it for him!

> *'The Lord has set the sun in the heavens*
> *but has said that he would dwell in thick darkness.*
> *I have built thee an exalted house,*
> *a place for thee to dwell in for ever.'* (vv. 12–13)

Solomon found it all impossible to explain, yet he had no
difficulty in calling his people to rejoice, indeed to exult,
because it had happened. God 'hidden and incomprehensible
had made himself known as the faithful one'. He had proved
himself again to be the God who has been, and will be, faithful
for ever to his covenant promise to Israel: The thought comes
up again and again. God *'has fulfilled what he promised'*. *'You
have kept your promise'* (v. 15; cf. 20, 24).

A New Avenue for Prayer

Since God had now taken over the temple as the place of his
name, Solomon immediately saw that he had thereby opened
up for his people a new avenue for worship, with new and
privileged possibilities of prayer. Early in Israel's history in
Canaan great significance was attached to any place where God
had appeared and spoken to one of the patriarchs. At such
places, they said, God 'had made his name known'. These
became places to which they could return again and again to
pray to him with the assurance that he would hear (cf. Gen.
13:4) One text in Exodus makes the promise: 'where I cause
my name to be honoured, I will come to you and bless you'
(Exod. 20:24). Moreover in chapter after chapter of the book
of Deuteronomy, the people of God are told that they must
worship God only at the 'dwelling place where he has put his
name' (12:58) or at the place which he has chosen as a 'dwelling
place for his name' (12:11; 14:23; 16:2,5,11; 26:2). Solomon
now claims that what has happened in the temple makes it
indeed this chosen and privileged dwelling place of his name.

Finally and forever, God's eyes, he believes, will be '*open towards this temple day and night*' so that he '*will hear the prayer your servant prays toward this place*' (v. 29).

Solomon may have had questions in his mind about how God could be thought of as dwelling both on earth and in heaven (v. 27) but he had no doubt that God could '*hear from heaven*' the prayers made here on earth (vv. 30,32,34). This temple was now a prayer centre opening up new assured possibilities for God's people in the realm of personal fellowship with God, even the God who can remain in heaven! Such fellowship will involve the asking and being heard that is called prayer, and the receiving of answers to such prayer made in God's name. Moreover this new way of prayer was opened up not only for those who prayed within the temple but for those who oriented themselves towards it (cf. vv. 30, 35, 38, 42, 44, 48) It covered the people of God wherever they were and whatever their need, and especially when their need was most acute.

Solomon in his prayer illustrated the unlimited range of human need under the pressure of which people could pray assured of God's help. He led the imagination of the congregation into several different cases in which such prayer, either within or towards the temple, might take place. When wronged people seek justice, when drought or plague blight their homesteads, when war brings its fearful misery, when people incurring guilt suffer punishment and even exile for their sins, let them turn mind and heart towards the Lord of Israel who has chosen the temple as his dwelling place, and cry to him out of the desperate situation. There is no fixed form for that cry to take, no rules for them to follow, except to spread out their hands towards the city and temple of God.

Solomon believed they could pray with complete certainty according to '*each days need*' (v. 59 N.I.V.) as it arose. He argues here that since God has fulfilled the one great promise of his coming into the midst to dwell with his people he will at the same time fulfil '*all the good promises*' (v. 56) he has made from the time of Moses to the time of David. The preface to his prayer of dedication is punctuated by pleas to God to '*keep what thou hast promised*' (vv. 25–6). The inspiration of all he has so far attempted in life has come from the promises he has

heard from God. Prayer, too, is for him simply asking God to
fulfil his promises.

We are meant to notice the repeated appeal, '*hear from
heaven,... and when you hear, forgive*' (vv. 30, 36, 39). Solomon
does not suggest which actual sins are to be forgiven. In the
presence of God he felt that we have to be forgiven for what
we are. Is it not true that when God becomes real to us, and we
know ourselves in his presence, we, too, experience a sense of
the sinfulness of our own persons? Can we ever, indeed, even
in our best attempts at goodness, get beyond the need to be
forgiven?

How near we often find ourselves to our own world of
experience when we read thoughtfully through these Old
Testament stories!. Two hundred years ago writing about this
passage of scripture a well known commentator remarked,
'Both tabernacle and temple were types of our Lord Jesus, or
of God *manifested in the flesh*; and he was and is the mediator
between God and man All prayer, to be acceptable, and to be
entitled to a hearing, must go to God *through him*. The human
nature of Christ is the temple in which *dwelt all the fullness of the
Godhead bodily*; therefore with propriety all prayer must be
offered to God through him' Such thoughts (and perhaps this
passage of Scripture) were in Jesus' mind when he told his
disciples that he was now opening up for them a new way of
prayer. It was to be opened up through his death, resurrection
and ascension to heaven. He called it prayer 'in my name' and
he promised that, from then on, with such a new avenue of
experience before them they would become bold and
confident in their praying. They could now enter his service
with conviction that nothing was now impossible for God. 'Until
now you have not asked for anything in my name. Ask and you
will receive and your joy will be complete' (John 16:24 N.I.V.).

Points for Further Thought and Discussion

We have interpreted Solomon's experience of worship in this incident as if it were very similar to our own. Is this justifiable? Did the men and women of the Old Testament experience in some way the actual presence of the One who comes to us in Christ? If so what were the differences between their experiences and ours?

Notice Solomon's vision of the 'thick darkness' at the heart of the also bright cloud of God's glory. Jesus has shown us that in God there is no darkness of which we need be afraid (cf. 1 John 1:5, John 8:12). Is it not still true that as we grow to understand and trust him that we find that there is in the wisdom of his ways a darkness that accompanies and veils what is essentially his love? A perceptive commentator of last century wrote of this passage: 'The eye of faith beholds in the darkness the glory of the Lord, in the light of the cross, the light of the world, through the dim veil of the flesh, the only begotten Son of God, full of mercy and grace.'

Solomon at times stood and at times kneeled as he 'spread out his hands towards heaven'. How much do you think our physical posture matters when we pray? Can we become too casual? Are there any rules?

On this quite unique occasion when Solomon and his congregation were remembering the coming of the cloud to the tabernacle, and praying for the same kind of blessing, God, in pure grace, came into their midst with the same presence and power as he had made the past event so significant and decisive. Does this unique happening give us any hint of what Jesus was telling us to expect when we fulfil his command at the Lord's Supper to 'do this in remembrance of me'?

'*When thou hearest, forgive.*' Read Ps. 51:5 and Matt. 15:18–19. Can you think of ways in which our innate sinfulness tends to spoil at times even our prayers, and our efforts for good?

Notes

The Cloud, the Presence and the Dwelling Place of God

In Old Testament experience and thought God was a gracious person, glorious in himself, above and beyond all that he had created. Yet he could come to meet his people (Exod. 25:22) and make himself present to them on earth. They could even speak of him as being both 'in the high and holy place, and also with him who is of a contrite and humble spirit' (Isa. 57:15). There is the thought of his giving us not only a transient presence (Jer. 14:8) but of choosing Zion as his 'dwelling place' on earth (Ps. 132:13f.; 1 Kings 8:13), even of his being 'enthroned' there (Ps. 48:2; Jer. 14:21, 17:12) upon the cherubim (Ps. 80:1)! Yet we are reminded often that such a throne is really simply his 'footstool' (1 Chron. 28:2; Ps. 99:5). Even in the sanctuary he is free to 'look down' from heaven (Deut. 26:15), and the sanctuary is thought of as being built, rather, for the *name* of the Lord. (cf. 1 Kings 8:27–30). That God chose a cloud to be a sign of his presence was of great significance to Solomon. It veiled his glory and represented his nearness, his hiddenness, and transcendence (cf. 1 Tim. 6:16).

The Ark

This was a rectangular chest of acacia wood which Moses was commanded to make during the wilderness journey (cf. Exod. 25:10–22; Deut. 10:1–5). It was to be placed within the tabernacle inside the veil that separated the holy of holies from the rest of the sanctuary. It contained the two tables of stone inscribed with the law of God and had on its lid two carved cherubim. From this 'mercy seat' God at times spoke to Moses. It had four rings at its base used for supporting stakes when it was carried about in the midst of the journeying people. Its presence in the tabernacle was a sign that God himself was present enthroned upon the cherubim (1 Sam. 4:4; cf. 2 Sam. 6:2). Its presence in the midst of the people on their journey was a sign that God was going with them on their way (Num. 10:33–36). When Joshua entered the promised land he sent the priests ahead bearing it with them into the river and the waters gave way before it to enable the people to pass over. During the early days of the conquest, Israel then carried it with them into battle, were strengthened by its presence in victory (Josh. 6:13) and defeat (Josh. 7:6). It was finally deposited in the re-erected tent at Shiloh. It was through a voice, appearing to come form the ark, that Samuel heard the voice of God speaking a word that, after years of decline, eventually brought about the great national renewal of Israel under David. Though the ark itself was abused, put in danger, and taken into temporary captivity by the Philistines, it was marvellously rescued and preserved (cf. 1 Sam. 5–6) till David, realising again the significance it could have for his national life after the occupation of Jerusalem, erected a tent in which it was installed (2 Sam. 6). There is no record of what happened to it when the temple was destroyed. Jeremiah regarded its disappearance at this stage in Israel's history as providential and progressive (Jer 3:16; cf. Job 1:21b).

CHAPTER VII

SOLOMON – HIS GREATNESS AND FALL
Chapter 9: 1 – 11:6

The Narrative

After his dedication of the temple Solomon continued to
win the respect of the whole world. The tenth chapter of
our account here is obviously written to evoke our
admiration and astonishment both over his earthly glory
and his share of divinely given wisdom, which drew the
Queen of Sheba to make her famous visit to Jerusalem,
and inspired her testimony to the greatness of the God of
Israel. The preceding ninth chapter, however, is on a
much more mundane level. God gave Solomon a severe
warning about what the future might contain for him.
We are therefore prepared to read about his fall as we
proceed to chapter eleven, and are given a clue to help
us to understand it..

Concern and Hope

These are two memorable chapters in 1 Kings which sketch
for us Solomon at the peak of his great career. In the eighth
chapter which we have already studied he is set before us as a
religious man, a lover of God's temple and worship. In the
tenth chapter he is described as a shining example of kingly
wisdom and splendour. Before we are allowed to move from
one summit of his career to the other, however, we have first
to read this very mixed ninth chapter with sometimes
uncomplimentary details of very mundane events. There is
the account of a quarrel he had with Hiram, his one – time

64

friend. Hiram had accused him of meanness because he had
pretended that a present he had offered him was more valuable
than it really was. There is also a reminder of how his craze for
building led him to conscript a slave-labour force. There is the
account of the care he lavished in completing the palace of
Pharaoh's daughter – his Egyptian wife!

We cannot help feeling that the author of this history has
quite deliberately arranged his chapters this way. He has
intentionally prefaced his final description of the greatness of
Solomon with these reminders of his weakness. This great king
so elevated before God and in the sight of the world, is indeed,
below the surface, struggling, amidst all the temptations and
weaknesses that flesh is heir to! These more unpleasant details
about Solomon are placed here in order to raise questions in
our minds about the final outcome, in terms of personal
destiny, of this man's earthly career. They are here also to
remind us of how firmly the grace of God upheld him in the
midst of his stubborn weakness.

We find the same questions raised in an even more pointed
way when we study the opening account in this chapter of how
'*the Lord appeared*' to Solomon '*a second time, as he had appeared
to him at Gibeon*' (9:2). We are taken back in thought to the
early vision in which Solomon was clearly told that he was to
be without equal, and was promised riches, honour, wisdom,
long life. In this second vision God expresses his pleasure that
in the building and dedication of the temple much of his hope
has been fulfilled, and encourages Solomon to follow the
example of David his father so that all the further promises
that have been lavished upon him might really come to pass
(9:3–5). After these encouraging words, however, a note is
struck that has not been sounded before in the promises given
by God about his own future, and that of those who will follow
on his throne – a note of deep concern. In the first vision,
greatness and success were promised to him without question
or hint of possible failure or tragedy. Now in the second vision
these promises are conditioned by a 'but' and an 'if'. We now
discover that God himself can see possible disaster marring
his own best hopes for this man, and thwarting what he is
promising.

It is as if God himself at the peak of Solomon's career now

saw before him the threat that his love could be ultimately
rejected. Might there not now be before him one, more like
Saul than David? He repeated, indeed, the kind of warning he
had given to Israel on the fateful day that Saul had been publicly
anointed king (Compare vv. 6–7 with 1 Sam 12:13–15, 24–25.)
He had never on any occasion spoken in this way to David.

Even though God does express such concern, the chief
purpose of this vision is to strengthen Solomon with '
encouragement and hope, for God himself is the 'God of hope'
(Rom. 15:13). God's aim is to win back this man to the love
that he had for himself during his early years (3:3) so that he
can finish with him the work they have begun together. The
vision is meant to be taken as an appeal rather than a warning.
It is a call to self examination – a call to pause and remember
the grace and goodness of God. What has his experience of
life and success in the service of God been doing to him? Was
he still giving God his heart as he gave him his service? Solomon
must put to himself the burning question: was the chief aim of
his life still '*to walk before me as David your father walked, with
integrity of heart and uprightness*' (9:4)?

'Solomon in all his glory'

Even after hearing the disturbing question God put to Solomon
in his second vision, we must not fail to appreciate, as fully as
we are meant to do, the lavish way in which God then quite
deliberately fulfilled all the promises he had made to him. As
his fame and influence grew he began to engage in vigorous
and successful commercial sea-faring activity. At the head of
the gulf of Aqaba in the Red Sea, he built ships and obtained
the assistance of Hiram's sea-men to help with their navigation.
Scholars vary in their views of the direction and length of their
trading routes. To go to Ophir for gold may have involved a
long arduous term at sea. (Some think they went as far as
India!) On the way to Ophir was Sheba, probably situated where
we have the modern state of Yemen. It was through the accounts
brought to her by her own sailors that the Queen of Sheba,
herself heard of Solomon. Astute in business matters she
probably realised that it could be profitable to contact him

and enter favoured trade arrangements with him. She had heard, too, that Solomon was world famous for his great wisdom. Such reports gave her a further purpose for wanting to meet him. In those days international life was sometimes marked by public contests in which people well known for their wisdom sometimes matched their wit and brain power with that of other famous people. She herself had a high estimation of her own ability and she wanted to test Solomon's wisdom with the questions and riddles with which, she felt, she might floor him.

In reading through the account of her visit we must not miss the mention of another motive, which in some way contributed to her desire to visit Jerusalem and which, as time passed, became more and more powerful. The queen desired to see Solomon because she had heard of his fame *'concerning the name of the Lord'* (10:1) This suggests that when Solomon found himself famed for his wisdom and had conferences with the men of all nations who were sent by their rulers to hear him (cf. 4:34), they also all heard something from him about why and how Israel, the Lord's people, had been given such blessing and prosperity, and insight into both human affairs and the natural world. A central aspect of his international wisdom was therefore his testimony to the Lord God of Israel, and he was not ashamed to make this clearly public in his 'press conferences'. We take this as something for which even at this later stage of his life we have to give to Solomon credit.

The visit was the occasion for an exceptionally brilliant display of both intellectual power and worldly wealth. The queen herself shone even in the great public contest of minds in which she plied Solomon with riddles and questions. The costliness and rareness of the gifts she brought with her *'very great retinue – with camels'*, made an outstanding impression on her host and his court. But *'nothing was hidden from the king which he could not explain to her'* (10:3) and she herself was overwhelmed by the palatial glory of Solomon's court, and the splendour in every detail of his household arrangements. The most important result of her visit, however is to be found in her own spontaneous testimony about it. God had opened her eyes to see through all the outward glitter of things to the glory of his presence and purpose with this people into whose midst she had come! Here in his *'eternal love'* (10:9) he has opened up a source of blessedness which can transform life for mankind! Here in the midst of the world where truth is often crushed, and might is right, a king has been given the wisdom and a nation the laws, that *'execute justice and righteousness'*! Here she has at last been given a decisive answer to all her anxious questions about the why and how of life. Here she has found a way of living that promises true stability and happiness. Her testimony to it is an evangelistic testimony. Here she has found blessing and been given a vision beyond the power of any human words to describe. Even the half had not been told her in all the praiseful reports that had drawn her to seek the presence of this king! Let others come, and they too will find!

Jesus himself, when he was preaching, thought of this story and wished that his own hearers in his day could begin to see in his own ministry what the Queen of Sheba had been granted to see and experience when she went to Jerusalem. To Jesus her ardent seeking and generous adulation of Solomon were a sign of the response that he himself, one far greater, deserved. Would that people around him be given eyes to see something of what that queen had seen in the kingship occupied by Solomon! He warned those who were rejecting him, that on the day of judgement, she, alongside the Ninevites who repented at the preaching of Jonah, would rise up and condemn them for their sloth, blindness, and coldness of heart (Luke 11:29–32).

And we too when we meet him and find what he has to give us, come to know that only a fraction of it has been told us in the words we have heard.

'One greater than Solomon'

The description of the splendour of Solomon's court and kingdom grows even more fulsome as we continue to read through the text before us. Nothing like Solomon's throne had ever been made for any other kingdom! Even the household articles in the Palace of the Forest of Lebanon were of pure gold! Silver was there regarded as of no value! His ships continued steadfastly to ply the seas and bring in exotic luxuries. Year by year the kings of the earth came and brought him presents: '*articles of silver and gold, garments and myrrh, spices, horses and mules*' (10:23)!

It seems obvious that throughout this chapter the writer himself is inspired by the same kind of enthusiasm about Solomon as was caught by the Queen of Sheba. He has seen in the grandeur of Solomon a preliminary earthly sketch of the Messianic kingdom promised by God. This is why he tends in his account to resort to the use of superlatives and to lapse into exaggeration in order to give an understandable emphasis to his point. Of course he is recording the facts of history, but at this crucial point in his description of Solomon's kingship he gives us no hint that there were more sombre and threatening aspects of his kingship of which he had to take account. He will deal honestly with these as his account goes on. At the moment they are kept out of sight. His purpose is to fix in our minds a speciaily impressive picture of the actual climax of Solomon's rule.

It has been customary for commentators on this passage (as also on like passages in the fourth chapter) to regard it is as written not simply to describe Solomon but also to lift up our minds and imagination to the reign of the coming Messianic king who would ultimately fulfil the promises given to Abraham when he was called out of Haran (Gen. 12:1ff.), and to David when God sent Nathan with the promise of the coming one from his loins whose throne would be established for ever (2 Sam. 7:8–16) 'The idealisation of Solomon's power and splendour here reaches its acme,' writes Skinner, 'There is something almost Messianic in the conception of a King of Israel, ruling the whole world, not by force of arms but by the spell of his personality, and the glamour of success which make him out as the favourite of heaven' We could add also that the secret of his power to rule is also to be found in the wisdom through which the whole world was drawn to him, and in which it found the meaning of life, and the way to live.

There can be little doubt that the sketch which we have here of Solomon's reign inspired Israel's great prophets, later on, to draw for us a remarkable picture of the glorious place which will be taken at the centre of the world's life by the redeemed people of God in their new eternal city after they have passed through their years of disappointment and humiliation (Isa. 2:1–5. Mic. 4: 1–4). In Isaiah chapter 60, there is a further description of all the kings of the earth bringing to Zion the 'wealth of the seas' and 'the riches of the nations' (including gold and incense from Sheba!) The 72nd Psalm, which seems to have been a prayer for one of the later kings of Judah, was also inspired by this description of Solomon, for it, too, gives us a picture of a great and glorious king in Zion receiving tribute from all the kings of the earth.

Such prophecies and prayers, inspired by this chapter on Solomon were often in the minds of the New Testament writers, and of Jesus himself. Signs of their fulfilment were given at his birth when the wise men from the East came to give him tribute, opened their treasures and offered him gifts. Before his death, the coming of the Greeks inspired the prophecy that through his death the solitary seed of his sacrificed life would 'bear a rich harvest' (John 12:24 NEB). 'Now shall the ruler of this world be cast out', he said, 'and I, when I am lifted up from the earth, will draw all men to myself' (John 12:32).

The writers and prophets who gave us such vivid descriptions of the coming glory of the Messianic kingdom could not have understood that what they were writing about could come to pass only if the same Messiah on whom God bestowed such glory was first crucified for the sins of those who were to bring him tribute. That Solomon had only such a partial understanding of the role he was to play in history must not however in any way diminish the appreciation of his achievement at this stage of his earthly career, or of the insight of the writer whose faith in God's promise made him look forward so earnestly to the future when he was writing about the present. Certainly we have to preach Christ crucified – a suffering saviour – and we have to call people to share and rejoice in the fellowship of his sufferings. But we must also affirm that the Christ we preach is going to attain and give to his people a glory of which we have only a mere faint foreshadowing in this picture of Solomon. Moreover, even if at present we suffer with him, we have already begun in the midst of our sufferings to have a foretaste of that coming glory.

Paul was describing our present life with Christ when he wrote to the Corinthians: 'All things are yours, whether Paul or Apollos or Cephas or the world or life or death or the present or the future – all are yours, and you are Christ's, and Christ is God's (1 Cor. 3:22).

Solomon – the Final Refusal

'*Happy are your wives*' (10:8) the Queen of Sheba had said in genuine tribute to Solomon's greatness. We are meant to feel some shock when we now at the beginning of the next chapter, read that they '*turned away his heart*' (11:3).

We are left in no doubt that this happened because Solomon by his own will and under the general pressure of the life he had to live, simply ignored the loving warning so clearly given in the second vision, (9:4) and allowed his heart to turn away in a direction other than God (11:2). It '*was not wholly true to the Lord his God as the heart of David his father*'. '*He did not wholly follow the Lord*' (11: 4–6). That he gave himself to follow false gods, finally Ashtoreth and Molech, was simply what inevitably happened after this great refusal to allow God himself completely to control him.

Other things certainly played their part – the wealth, the sensuality (700 wives!), the luxury, but he is not specifically condemned for allowing himself too much ease or careless indulgence. He is condemned for allowing his heart to settle on what is less than God alone. Jeremiah has reminded us that as human beings we can have only one object of trust. If we trust in 'man' or 'the arm of flesh' then our heart inevitably 'departs from the living God' and we are 'cursed' rather than 'blessed' (Jer. 17: 5–8). It was because this disorientation of heart happened with Solomon at the climax of his career that he was so easily seduced by his wives and drawn into idolatry.

We must not underestimate Solomon. The promises of God sent him on the path to greatness, and his own early response to them was genuine. What he achieved in the service of the Word of God was magnificent. Of course the personal faults and mistakes of policy become obvious at times. Yet in face

of many real difficulties he took God at his word, and pleased
him. Nor must we allow ourselves to dwell too much on the
scandal with which this great career was brought to an end.
The author of the Book of Chronicles thought his
contribution to the history of Israel so great that he omits
any mention of his final days of shame. What we are meant to
think about is, rather, the tragedy. God never meant it –
between himself and his beloved Solomon – and it happened!
This is what life can bring into the rather more obscure and
less important sphere in which we ourselves live today. We
never imagined that it might happen – and yet it happens –
the absurd and the unthinkable! What we are meant also to
think about as we continue the story is that eventually God
dealt with it and used it so marvellously, triumphantly and
justly in the end and with infinite patience and wisdom. The
question comes back to us: are we ourselves trusting him today
to do the same?

Points for Further Thought and Discussion

In chapter 9:4–7 God made the fulfilment of his promises to Solomon and his successors dependent on obedience. In the New Testament, obedience is no longer a *condition* of being blessed, but is expected as a *result*. Why is there this difference?

Early in this twentieth century it seemed to many Christians that the whole world, under the spread of Christ's gospel was going to become gradually christianised, and Christ universally acknowledged as Lord. Though such hope has not been realised what facts and signs are there in the world today that point to his coming glory?

On what kind of issues does the 'wisdom' taught by Jesus (e.g. the Sermon on the mount) and embodied in his life, conflict with the wisdom of the world today? How can the church seek to convince the world of its worth and show its attractiveness?

The queen of Sheba showed no restraint in expressing her joy over what she had experienced and seen in Solomon's court, and no hesitation in saying that it could be found nowhere but in the city of the God of Israel. Has her example relevance for us today?

Solomon loved many foreign women (11:1). What are the chief essential differences between this kind of love and that described in 1 Corinthians chapter 13?

What are the temptations and pressures within the modern world that are most likely to 'turn away our heart' from the Lord? Should warnings about such a personal danger be given clearer place than at present in the teacing of the Church?

Notes

Solomon as a type of Christ
The New Testament disciples of Jesus found written in the Old Testament many prophecies of Christ and of what was to

happen to themselves as a Church. They found particular events of his earlier career, of his life, death and resurrection foretold. Sometimes the prophecies were given in verbal utterances delivered by inspired prophets. At other times they found such prophecies given through features of the national history of the Old Israel, in incidents that happened to persons, especially to their prophets and kings, and in aspects of their established institutions such as their cult priesthood. The exodus from Egypt, for example, was recognised as a prophecy of the kind of deliverance Christ was to accomplish for them as he himself went through death and rose again and as they experienced their salvation through him. God thus seems to have occasionally embodied in the history of his people events which would foreshadow things to come, thus making the old history symbolic or 'typical' of the history that was to be fulfilled when Christ came, to use a phrase of Paul (1 Cor 10:11 N.E B.).

As we read through the Old Testament we are meant to notice how such symbolic pictures or 'types' occur now and then, foreshadowing the career of the coming Messiah. Jesus himself taught Nicodemus that the lifting up by Moses of the serpent in the wilderness (John 3:14, Nu. 21:8ff.) was a type of what would happen to him on the cross. He interpreted the passages in Isaiah about a suffering 'servant' of God (Isa. 41:1–4; 49:1–6; 50:4–9; 52:13–53:12) which read like the description of a contemporary unknown suffering prophet, to be a prophecy of what was to happen to himself. We ourselves, following this example have in this chapter interpreted this picture of Solomon's glory, with its quite deliberate touches of exaggeration to be read also within the context of the whole Old Testament as foreshadowing another partial aspect of the coming Messiah.

One feature of this picture of his earthly supremacy specially emphasised is his wisdom (10:24). Here is where the Gospel excels. In a world which by its wisdom cannot know God, the hidden wisdom that 'God destined for our glory' before time began, 'has now been revealed to us by the Spirit' (1 Cor 2:7–10).

Almug Wood

Commentators express doubt about what tree this was, because there is doubt about the location of Ophir. If this place was in India, there is a likelihood that it was red sandalwood.

CHAPTER VIII

SOLOMON, REHOBOAM, AND JEROBOAM – THE TRAGIC SUCCESSION
1 Kings 11:7–12:33

The Narrative

Everything we read in this section of the text before us is depressing and tragic. Solomon is no longer courted by the world. His rule at home is troubled by serious opposition, and his character degenerates. A prophet announces the ultimate break-up of his kingdom. This is brought about by the folly of Rehoboam his son and successor. Jeroboam, now over the rival half-kingdom, uses the liberty and power entrusted to him to defy the Lord. Yet God continues to give signs of his power creatively to triumph over evil.

Change and Decay – Towards Fulfilment

It is worth while reviewing the remarkable change that is now beginning to take place in the strategy adopted by God in controlling the history and destiny of his people.

In the first few chapters of the book of Samuel we read about a new beginning that took place under Samuel in the history of the tribes of Israel after the period of the Judges. It led to a gradual yet growing improvement in every aspect of the affairs of the nation. There were occasional set-backs, as for example in Saul's persecution of David, and in David's own sin over Bathsheba with its devastating results, but the whole story has been of lasting and consolidated progress in understanding God and his purposes. The history of these times recorded for us in the books of Samuel and Kings up to the point we have so far reached has been written with a hopeful forward look. The remarkable prophecy of Nathan to David, in 2 Samuel 7, has encouraged us to feel that God has been positively and graciously at work here, to bring about the fulfilment of his promises. He has been steadily moving history in a progressive way. The glorious description of Solomon's kingship confirmed our hopeful outlook.

Now, however, from the beginning of the eleventh chapter of Kings a bewildering and devastating change in the direction of Israel's history takes place. Jealousy and arrogance among the tribes takes precedence over brotherhood and godly tradition. The kingdom is split in two. Though civil war is avoided, each section is led by men devoid of faith or vision. As one scholar puts it: 'the rebellion of the ten tribes was the most important and pregnant event in the history of Israel since it became an independent state'. The prevailing atmosphere and tone of religious, political and social life seems to degenerate. As we read through the coming chapters, question marks appear over what seemed to be encouraging certainties. The threat of future decadence seems to replace the hope of further progress.

The history of Israel under the kings to whom we now begin to be introduced, is to be of further recession instead of advance. It is true that decadence is occasionally broken by the appearance of green shoots promising a fruitful new start. But these are soon blighted. The writer obviously intends that before these happen, we should prepare ourselves to read of the final disasters that will in the end come to both kingdoms.

Yet nothing is irretrievable with God. He can wait. Men must and will, in the long term, become subject to him. If Israel will not follow his call in one direction, a new way will be taken. We find him even in the age of these kings preparing for an age to come, when he will finally manifest his glory and reveal his power. Though both Judah and Israel enter a period of swift change and decay, this very period becomes the age in which great prophets begin to appear and flourish. They are always forward looking. They teach not only what will meet the needs of their own age but also point Israel's faith to look forward to greater things than even their past promised.

Solomon's Last Days

God had up till now helped Solomon by restraining any opposition that might have spoiled the success that had so far marked his rule. Yet it had happened that even when he came to his throne, two enemies had positioned themselves within the extreme borders of his kingdom. They were Hadad, the Edomite, and Rezon in Damascus. Both had been bitter over the wrongs they felt that David had inflicted on those to whom they had belonged. They had tried to stir up strife with local guerrilla forces but so far God had curbed the dissension and disorder they could have caused. Now, however, a radical change came about in Solomon's fortunes. The international community lost interest in him, and serious unrest grew in the provinces that David his father had annexed with force. Hadad and Rezon are now named as 'adversaries' (11: 14, 23) raised up by God not only to cause trouble but also to be signs to Solomon that the world around him was no longer on his side. Their increasing activity and power no doubt served also to block his caravan routes and further affected his economy.

Even though God is spoken of as 'raising up' such adversaries to execute his judgement on Solomon we do not need to imagine that in any way he stirred up or excited the hatred and desire for revenge that brought about his downfall. He 'tempts no one to evil' (James 1:13) He simply slackened the restraints on the bitterness and contempt that were already there and that had their origin in what is alien to himself. God also slackened the restraints by which he had withheld Solomon himself from the folly and evil to which we are all so naturally inclined. The great king's 'wisdom' in the government of Israel's affairs had of course always been the result of the sensitivity with which he had been able to enter into the motives and feelings of others, of God-given tact and self-denial. Now he let Solomon freely take his own way, break through the restraints imposed by his former godliness, take his fill of purely self-centred 'love', and at the same time plunge into the way of folly.

Moreover God ceased to curb the dissension and disorder which had always been there, even at the height of his popularity, ready to find its expression when it was provoked.

We noted earlier his power to make wise judgements in
ordering the affairs of his kingdom. This marked the early
stages of his reign. He lost this ability, and he himself was
responsible for giving the third adversary mentioned in our
text the opportunity to work havoc among his subjects.

There was at Millo a gap in the city wall. It had been left by
David. To build it up involved rough toil. But in Jerusalem
with its high standard of living labour was scarce and expensive.
Solomon resorted to importing from the North labour gangs
who were willing to put their hands to the rough and hard
labour. It was a grossly unwise move. They came from a now
deprived area and found themselves poorly paid and despised
in the midst of all Solomon's splendour and extravagance.
Outstanding among them was Jeroboam, a man of exceptional
energy and ability. Solomon, with his usual keen eye for spotting
investment, trusted him, and put him fully in charge. Since he
was a widow's son he looked upon him as a deserving case for
advancement (11:26–28). He did not realise that Jeroboam
himself was seething with the very anti-South resentment of
which he himself was beginning to be afraid! Dislike for the
supremacy of Judah 'was in the blood of so young and powerful
a man as Jeroboam, and it needed not much to excite it', writes
one commentator. God had allowed 'wise' Solomon to slip into
a whole series of mistakes.

As well as removing restraints that had brought peace to
Solomon's province, God himself actively entered the human
situation to bring about the decisive break-up. Through the
prophet Ahijah he sent the word that gave Jeroboam ultimately
the power to tear the kingdom in two. God had read Jeroboam's
heart and offered him what he desired (11:29–39).

We will discover later that Jeroboam even at this stage must
have been a man without faith in God. His later behaviour
shows that he paid little heed to the offer of God to make his
own earthly career as splendid and fruitful as David's. But it
did register in his mind that this strange man who accosted
him in the field might have uncanny insight into fate or
fortune. He must have spoken about it to others. Possibly he
took the message as an encouragement to show his hand and
stir up trouble. Solomon must have heard of the Word of God
that threatened to bring his once glorious kingdom to such a

tragic end. God did not bring about the coming disaster while Solomon was alive, but he was forced to live under its impending shadow.

It is one of the saddest features of his last days that when he heard what had been said to Jeroboam, instead of seeking God's forgiveness his thoughts turned to murder and revenge, and Jeroboam had to flee (11:40). Was it a lingering fear of the Lord that made Solomon afraid to lay his hand upon the equally guilty prophet? 'No-one can serve two masters,' said Jesus, 'either he will hate the one and love the other, or he will be devoted to the one and despise the other' (Matt. 6:24).

Rehoboam

As the reign of Rehoboam began, the relations between the South and the North had reached their breaking point. The North had become deprived of enterprise, resources and opportunities for fruitful work. The South, around Jerusalem, even in its fading magnificence, had something left over from the glory brought to it by Solomon. There was wealth, the means to gain and enjoy it, and to employ others in its pursuit. If there was to be a future for a united kingdom there was need for a ruler who could remember their common tradition under the redeeming love of one Lord, their blood brotherhood, and the past faithfulness of one tribe to another within the family of Abraham.

The older men around the court were troubled in conscience about the possible division, feared the unrest and saw the danger ahead. Therefore when Rehoboam asked their advice, they reminded him not only that brotherhood and mutual service were meant to prevail in Israel, but that the king himself was raised up and appointed by God for service as well as for rule. '*If you will be a servant to this people today and serve them... they will be your servants for ever*' (12:7).

But around the palace and court in Jerusalem there had grown up as companions of the young prince a generation unsympathetic to the needs of the deprived. Their advice was fatal. Crush all protest and ban demonstration! Teach them obedience by making their load heavier! If Solomon had failed to subdue them with whips, let Rehoboam use scorpions! (12:9–11)

As we read of the gathering at Shechem to appoint their future king we are meant to note the secularity that now prevailed within the nation's life. The issues before them were critical and decisive for their future. Yet no priest was invited, no prayer was offered, no reference at all was made to God and his will, even by the elders. Can we not find a clue to the personal arrogance that marked Rehoboam's approach to his subjects precisely in this lack of that sense of the living God that inevitably brings humility? And can we trace his sheer folly to Solomon's neglect of his education? As a father he must have failed to communicate to his son the wisdom that he knew so well, and taught so convincingly in the days of his greatness.

The writer clearly demonstrates that it was Rehoboam's pride and stupidity that brought about the split in the kingdom. Nevertheless he affirms that God himself took control of everything that happened and worked his will through it all. Rehoboam did not listen to the people, *'for it was a turn of affairs brought about by the Lord, that he might fulfil his word'* (v. 15) God is always Lord over what happens. He knows and directs the course of events. Yet each person involved has to make real and crucial decisions about his or her own part in what is taking place. God is always ready in his grace to relax and change his own course if his people in their freedom will repent and change theirs. Rehoboam is fatally responsible even for what God is seen to have already decreed.

We read on to find the wretched young king making two foolish last attempts to regain what had been lost. He should have understood that Adoniram, whom Solomon had used to oversee his forced labour, was the last man who should have accompanied him on a peace mission designed to heal the differences that had arisen, and maintain Israel's unity. Probably, however, he was the only man in his council who was familiar with the North, and he had to use somebody. Adoniram was stoned to death, and the king himself had to flee. Then shamefully he decided on civil war – the killing of brother by brother! It was by God's mercy that when they advanced to begin the fighting, God sent the prophet Shemaiah with the

Word '*This thing is from me*' and '*they hearkened to the Word of the Lord*' (12:24)

Jeroboam

We are given no hint as to why God chose this man, Jeroboam, to be the first ruler of the newly formed kingdom of Northern Israel, and lavished on him such fulsome promises. At no stage in his subsequent career as king does he seem to have been the kind of man who would ever want to respond to God's invitation to '*walk in my ways and do what is right in my eyes*' so that he could found a dynasty '*as enduring as the one I built for David*' (11:38, N.I.V.). It may be that in the very early days of his career, when Ahijah the prophet encountered him in the field, he showed a real inclination to become a servant of God. But if so, something very shattering and disillusioning must have happened to him during his years of waiting in exile in Egypt. When he came back to Israel he showed not a trace of respect for the truth of his fathers in the faith. Why God chose him to be the first king of the separated tribes, is one of the insoluble mysteries of the Bible. (like the question why Jesus chose Judas). It may be that God simply had to take the best he could find around him in the situation in order to get on with the job in the time he had at his disposal. Jeroboam may have been the most promising and capable person in the midst of a fairly decadent social milieu.

It is characteristic of the grace and reliability of God, that in spite of the fact that there was so little response from the man before him, he nevertheless kept his word, and opened up the promised opportunity. Jeroboam, of course, was there in Jerusalem immediately Solomon died, expecting what had been foretold him. We will discover as we come to know him better, that he believed human destiny to be in the hands of a blind but inevitable fate. His experience of life had taught him that people like God's so-called prophets possessed uncanny insight and could tell fortunes. He wanted to be at hand, on the spot, in case it happened – and it did! Here he was – king of Israel!

He was shrewd and calculating – quite unlike his impulsive
and stupid rival, Rehoboam in Judah. He knew that his hold
on his kingdom was fragile. His first concern was to attend
to the defence of his realm by fortifying two cities. And as
for religion – if Rehoboam and his associates around
Jerusalem had grown careless about this, not so Jeroboam!
He realised the vital importance such a pursuit could have
within the life of his new 'nation'. He was afraid that if he
did not encourage a locally centred religion his people
would ultimately be drawn back to the temple of Jerusalem.
They would then transfer their political loyalty there too
and he would lose. Therefore they must have a more
localised religion. It must be as simple and native as possible,
and they must have plenty of it too! He would devise and
control it himself. He no doubt worked hard at the problem,
and consulted experts. Finally he came up with a form of
worship designed especially for two shrines of central
importance in his kingdom – one at Bethel and the other at
Dan In each of these temples the thoughts of the people
would no longer be centred on the ark as a symbol of the
presence of the invisible Lord. Such a religion might make
them long to be back in the Jerusalem temple. Their
devotion must be centred rather on the image of a young
bull calf made of gold. Such golden bulls were the kind of
image familiar to those who worshipped Baal everywhere.
Jeroboam, however, intended them to remind the
worshipper, rather, of the Lord himself. *'Behold your gods, O
Israel who brought you up out of Egypt'* (12:28) It was a crude
attempt at the mixture of religions that we today call
'syncretism'. Having dressed his falsehood up in the
trappings borrowed from truth, he did his best to make
people think they had something as genuinely from their
fathers as the cult at Jerusalem – only here everything was
more simple, natural and appealing to their senses.

To make sure that the whole religious activity of the nation
was kept within his own realm of control, he built official local
'high places' for the open air rites loved by the people, but
hated by the prophets. He appointed religious feasts to rival
those traditionally held in Jerusalem, and of course as many
priests as were required.

We are to note that '*this thing became a sin*' (12:30) How great a sin will be made clear as its consequences unfold. The Northern kingdom gradually grew more and more degenerate. Centuries later as it moved on towards its final dissolution and the exile of its people, we still read of king after king that 'he did not turn away from the sins of Jeroboam'

In the case of both Solomon and Rehoboam it is made clear by the writer that even in their deeds of dissoluteness and folly, the hand of God was there controlling and directing them. No such thought is suggested when he speaks of Jeroboam devising and introducing such a perverse and false religion. Here the evil is so hateful to God and so alien to his nature and will that he does not seek to control it or work it into his redeeming purposes. He seeks only to annihilate it.

Points for Further Thought and Discussion

After reading through this section make a list of the chief factors causing the decline and break up of Israel as a nation at this time. What was chiefly responsible? What could have prevented it? What relevance has this for us as a Church and a nation today?

The Lord raised up three adversaries to disturb and anger Solomon in his latter days. Proverbs 16:7 affirms that when our ways please the Lord, he will make even our enemies live at peace with us. Does God still act in this way in modern international and personal life? If so how should it affect us?

This story illustrates a generation gap. Solomon failed to educate Rehoboam in what he knew. Rehoboam and his contemporaries failed to accept the advice of older wise men. Read the fourth commandment. And also Malachi 4: 5–6. Why is the generation gap today serious? And how can we put it right?

Jeroboam in his day, simplified his religion because he was afraid it was too difficult to be popular. Do we tend today to make the demands of our Christianity less stringent and its doctrine more simple than they really are in order to make it more popular, and in the process do we tend to destroy it?

After blaming the split up of the kingdom on the folly and pride of men, the writer, nevertheless ,reminds us (cf. v.15 and vv. 11–12) that in the midst of, and in spite of, all this wickedness, God himself was at work to fulfil his word. Read Genesis 50:20 and Acts 2:23. Though *we* may be guilty God can overrule, yet this does not remove our responsibility or our freedom. Think how this fact can both comfort us, and act as a warning to us in our struggle to serve him.

Notes

The Prophetic Sign
God often made his will come to pass by making his messenger

or prophet announce what he was going to do. The utterance of the spoken word was effective. When Elijah announced the famine, it happened (1 Kings 17:1ff.). Sometimes, however, God used signs as well as words. When Elisha cleansed the well at Jericho, he threw salt into it, as well as speaking a word. (2 Kings 2:21). Prophets often sought to bring about what they prophesied not only by the words they uttered but by symbolic action (e.g. Isa. 20:2; Jer. 13:1; Ezek. 4:1). In the incident in this chapter the tearing up of Ahijah's new garment is to be regarded as being not just symbolic, but also as being instrumental in bringing about what it symbolised.

The Decline in Public Religion
One commentator brings to our notice that in all important national gatherings of Israel to decide important issues their first concern was to ensure the presence and blessing of God. When Joshua gathered the tribes at Shechem, 'they presented themselves before God' (Josh. 24:14). At Mizpah, under Samuel, they were called solemnly to 'present yourselves before the Lord' (1 Sam. 10:19). When David was made king at Hebron, it was sealed with a 'covenant... before the Lord' (2 Sam. 5:3). At the anointing of Solomon 'they worshipped and performed sacrifices to the Lord' (2 Chron. 29:20–1). We are meant to note in this chapter, that the rulers have so lost their sense of God that there is no reference to him at all. There is irony in the fact that it was Jeroboam the agnostic who seemed to be aware of the influence that some form of religion could exercise in public life.

JEROBOAM UNDER THE WORD OF GOD

I Kings 13: 1 – 14:20

The Narrative

In describing the reign of Jeroboam, the writer passes over the wars and other events of his rule that might have then seemed important, and concentrates on three fascinating stories about him as a person. They each help us to find a consistent picture of how his mind worked, of what he felt about life, and how he reacted to the Word of God. One of them, in passing, introduces us to the kind of personal intercourse which could take place in the 'schools of the prophets' which were beginning then to flourish in both Judah and Israel. The final episode clearly reveals the cause, and the full extent of the tragedy with which his life ended.

Jeroboam, Condemned, Healed and Rebuked.

We have here a deliberately drawn contrast. On the great day when the Jerusalem temple was dedicated, Solomon was there standing by the altar as the glory of the Lord filled the house of the Lord, and he uttered his divinely inspired and memorable words about worship and prayer. Here was Jeroboam on one of his great days, no doubt inaugurating one of his new religious festivals in defiant opposition, and the voice of a 'man of God' proclaimed loudly that his altar would one day receive the only sacrifice it was fit for – the dead and rotten corpses of the pagan priests he had appointed in his realm to spread false worship!

It is possible that Jeroboam as a youth in Jerusalem had been present himself and had been trying to capture for his own temple something of the religious aura of that great former occasion as he posed himself there to burn incense *standing by the altar.* He had good reason to be satisfied and hopeful. His religious revolution had been successful. His temple even at distant Dan was attracting pilgrims. There had been no sign of public reaction against his new set-up from among the devout in his land, or even from 'the men of God' around him. Some of the local prophets even allowed their sons to take part in the celebrations. The interruption was therefore all the more shattering because it was completely unexpected. Some commentators, anxious to eliminate unnecessary miracles, suggest that the sudden emotional shock of it brought on a complete paralysis of the arm which to onlookers, seemed to wither and become stiff – a possible stroke.

We must admire the courage of the prophet from the South. He would have been subjected to mob violence if the king's command to seize him had been immediately obeyed. But amid the confusion, an earthquake 'split apart' the altar and scattered its very ashes!

We are left to put our own interpretation on the momentary change that came over Jeroboam. Why did he suddenly and with apparent meekness ask for the visitor's help in prayer? It does not fit the context to suppose that he was at last turning to God even momentarily in true faith and repentance. We believe that in the request he made for prayers he was as distant from God as he had ever been in his mood of greatest cynicism. His request to the prophet was carefully worded. There was not a trace of repentance. Let him pray to the '*Lord your God*' (13:6). In a moment of fear he was merely grasping at the chance that people such as these prophets had secret ways and special powers to make things happen.

The parting message which the prophet delivered to Jeroboam was as powerful and pointed as his blunt introductory confrontation at the altar had been. The king had felt grateful for the healing of his arm, and perhaps thought that the offer of hospitality and a gift might help to soften the wrath of the powers that had caused the earthquake at his altar. His adversary was contemptuous in his refusal. '*If*

you give me half your house, I will not go in with you' (13:8, cf. Gen.
14:22–23). He left, as he had been ordered, and chose an
unknown way home. Jeroboam, unrepentant, was left, however,
with much to think about – the sign of the ruined altar, the
miraculous healing of his arm, and the final word of God's
continuing displeasure.

The Word of God, Betrayed and Vindicated

Locally, however, there was a quite unexpected and sensational
development. *'An old prophet'* (13:11) lived nearby. He himself
had never raised any protest against Jeroboam's golden calves
and did not share in the intolerance of his paganism which he
knew to prevail in some of the schools of the prophets. Indeed
the action which we will now witness indicates that he was
friendly towards the king. When he heard of the happenings
in the shrine, and the younger prophet's parting words of
contempt, he followed him with desperate speed, and with
despicable guile, pretending that he had a message from the
Lord, countermanding his order to fast. He persuaded him to
come back to his home to break his God given vow of
abstinence and to eat at his table.

The story is told in such a way as to leave us free to put our
own interpretation on the old man's feelings and motives. That
he had lived so long and so near to Jeroboam's shrine, without
any sign of protest in the name of God, seems to indicate that
he had lost touch with the faith and ideas that had once
inspired him. Renegade priests and pastors can too easily
become cynical over the zeal of those who remind them too
acutely of how far they have fallen! He must have felt himself
rebuked by what had happened and he may have resented the
intrusion of a brother prophet into his area without even a
passing visit. Whatever his motives, his behaviour was cruel
and vicious. He knew how to use the language of a father-in-
God to trap his inexperienced younger brother: *'I also am a
prophet as you are, and an angel of the Lord spoke to me by the word of
the Lord saying, "Bring him back with you into your house that he
may eat bread"'* (13:18). There can be little doubt that it was to
his immense satisfaction when he found his treachery working.

He had been able to prove to himself that these enthusiastic young prophets from the South were weaker and more liable to yield to temptation than their bold and brave words made them seem at first to be. Even the king when he heard of the turn-around, (so easily worked!) could take comfort in the fact that the parting public rebuke which had stung so badly, was mere empty rhetoric and that perhaps the prophet's whole message had been phoney after all!

We ourselves are meant to feel acutely the intense tragedy – that a great day's work for God should end so questionably, and that a servant of God so courageous and transparently sincere should be so easily duped. The tragedy is deepened when we hear the death sentence against him, which came through the old prophet at the very moment when he broke his sacred vow. (13: 21–22) We wish that his life at least could have been spared but in those days life was hard and judgements were harsh.

But now there happens one of the simplest, most subtle, powerful and effective miracles in the whole of Holy Scripture at the exact moment when its message could be most transparent. God broke into the tragic situation and quite suddenly set right everything that had seemed to have broken down. Moreover, it was all done through two dumbly obedient animals tamed for a few hours from all viciousness or fear. The lion having made his kill and executed the hand of judgement, stood for hour after hour alongside the ass beside the body as if they felt the shame of what had happened, and the public, amazed, passed by and spread the report of it. Here was God doing honour both to the word of the prophet he had sent from the South and the word he had spoken through him against Jeroboam. The prophet had certainly sinned and his sin had been punished – to vindicate the sanctity of God's command. Yet God had pardoned him, blotting out the remembrance of his tragic fault and was now vindicating the word he had spoken against the altar and the rebellious king.

The message of the whole incident suddenly came home to the mind and conscience of the old prophet. He underwent a marvellously repentant conversion of attitude. He hastened to give the dead brother the burial with which he knew God wanted now to honour him, and he could think of no greater

honour for himself than to share his tomb when he himself
died (13:31).

The whole incident, in the end, proved to be a word for
Jeroboam. The king could not have escaped knowing all that
had happened, and must have heard the public testimony
which the old man made to his sons: '*that the Word of the Lord
against the altars in Bethel and against the houses of the high places
in Samaria shall surely come to pass*' (13:32). Yet '*Jeroboam did not
turn from his evil way*' (13:33). Indeed, he plunged with renewed
vigour into the defiance that led to the downfall of his house.

The Final Indictment

How patient God has been with Jeroboam demonstrating his
mercy as well as his judgement, dealing firmly, even severely,
but leaving the door open for him to think again and change
his attitude. God has been waiting. It has depended on the
king. In the final episode, to which we now turn, the
atmosphere has seemed to change. Unmitigated defiance now
meets with unmitigated severity on the part of God himself.
God now consigns this man to the outer darkness and loss
which are to be his fate. Jeroboam is now identified with 'dung'
fit only to be burned, and his name is now to be made to stand
in the history of Israel for everything in God's sight that is
alien, and hateful to goodness and holiness (14:10–16). It is
the final words of condemnation of Jeroboam and his house
pronounced by the prophet Ahijah that reveal to us why God
was forced finally to pronounce such a verdict on him. '*You
have done more evil than all who lived before you. You have thrust me
behind your back*' (14:9 NIV). Time and again in his career God
had been there before this king, time and again appealing,
offering him friendship and seeking his trust. Consistently and
without a trace of hesitation on Jeroboam's part he had met
contempt, aversion and hatred. This perverse reaction had
been made in the face of God's patient love and hope with
deliberate purpose and will, never unknowingly or even
carelessly, but always with the intention that it should insult
and hurt. It is sometimes pointed out that the Old Testament
has no doctrine of everlasting punishment. But it does speak

of an 'everlasting contempt' (Dan 12:2) and it gives us the
example of Jeroboam. A notable Anglican Bishop, expressing
his belief that there was a hell, at the same time affirmed that
no one would ever go there except those to whom God had
first clearly opened his arms of love and was then deliberately
rejected.

Solidarity and Tragedy

Everything that happens in the last years of Jeroboam's life
seems irretrievably tragic. His eldest son, a favourite with
everyone in the land, becomes mortally ill. We can understand
why, when it happened, the king's thoughts, turned to Ahijah,
'the one who told me I would be king' (14:2 N.I.V.). The same man,
at the same time had said things that were great and exciting
about the dynasty that was to follow him on his throne. Might
he not be able to recall what was said? *'He will tell.... what shall
happen to the child'*, he said to his wife when he sent her as his
messenger. He has no thought of pleading for supernatural
help for his boy. Like those who today seek simply the
knowledge of their predetermined future from the stars, he
seeks from Ahijah only his fortune! At least to know it will steady
his nerves, quell some of his anxieties, and enable him to gain
strength to face it.

The thought of facing Ahijah, however, had put him in
tension. He had a wistful longing to go to the man himself.
But he was too proud. How could he maintain his leadership
and dignity if he himself broke the laws that forbade his people
to go on pilgrimage to Jerusalem? Perhaps, too, there was the
fear that in any close encounter with Ahijah he might find
himself challenged by a god he did not want to face. He decided
to escape the personal encounter by sending his wife. He would
avoid the shame and the public scandal by sending her in
disguise. Even the gift she must take would be so modest that
none would suspect it to come from the royal purse (14:2–3).

We are forced by the writer to feel something of the agony
and shame that came upon this poor woman in her attempt to
please him. She was no doubt even more anxious and
despairing than he. She obeyed and respected his ways, and

suddenly she finds herself exposed to shame and confusion.
'*Come in, wife of Jeroboam; why do you pretend to be another?*' (14:6).
She finds herself forced to become not only the messenger of
doom to her husband but also the bearer of death to her own
child for it will be as she crosses the threshold of her home
that God will take him to himself! The tragedy at this point is
becoming intense. This woman seems to be suffering not for
her own sins but for those of Jeroboam! And if, as was quite
possible, she herself was truly a godly woman simply trying to
do the duty of a good wife, she suffered all the greater torment
by being bound up with him in the situation.

The tragedy deepens when we think of the child. The
suggestion of the passage is that his young heart was right with
God and that he kept God's covenant for we read that he was
the only member of Jeroboam's family to receive a good burial
(14:13). There is a legend that he had used his authority to
remove sentries who prevented people from going to Jerusalem
to worship, and had even gone there himself. He was beloved
by the people!

How realistic the Bible is, especially in its early stories, about
the suffering that can come to innocent people, especially
because they are bound up through family ties with those who
incur and deserve judgement because of their sins. Sometimes
those who write the history, as in this passage, deliberately bring
out the fact that innocent children can often suffer for the
sins of their parents. It is emphasised, for example, that the
child of David and Bathsheba died under the judgement that
came upon his father (2 Sam 13:14). Sometimes the historians
bring out the fact that the anguish of the tragedy in which
both innocent and guilty are involved is felt more acutely by
the innocent than by the guilty party. It was the godly wife of
Phinehas, one of the stupid and hardened high Priests of Israel
who bore most heavily the shame of desolation of heart
involved in the downfall of Israel and the loss of the Ark, for
which her husband was largely responsible (cf. 1 Sam 4:19 –
22). We too have to face the fact that even today there are
many people around who feel they have cause to be grieved
for what they inherited from their parents. The people of Israel
were at times deeply perplexed that the iniquity of the fathers'
could thus be 'visited upon the children' (Exod 20:5) and when

they were in exile in Babylon many of them were so bitter over the fact that they were suffering for sins they themselves had not committed that they coined a cynical proverb, The fathers have eaten some grapes and the children's 'teeth are set on edge'.

Solidarity and Salvation

God has a purpose in exposing so often and so realistically in the stories of the Old Testament the vicious and persistent hold which human sin has over us, and the bitterness and perplexities of the tragic situations that ordinary human beings are so often involved in because of our sin. As he unfolds the story of salvation he wants us at the same time to become more and more aware of the intricate and desperate nature of the plight out of which he has come to save us. He wants us, moreover, to appreciate the glorious and miraculous nature of the answer he is going to give to the questions raised in our minds by such appalling and irretrievable human tragedy. That answer was of course finally and triumphantly given in the life, death and resurrection of Jesus and will be finally sealed when he comes again to put all things right, and solve every human riddle at his judgement seat. It is worth while, however, before we pass from this particular instance of our problem to point out how God, in thus revealing our human plight, set about answering the problems raised by it.

There are, of course, in the Old Testament itself very many stories of individuals who by faith in the Christ who was to come endured and overcame all the tragedies and difficulties with which they were continually threatened in living their lives. We have an impressive list of some of them in the eleventh chapter of Hebrews. There are several passages in Old Testament history which can especially help us to understand the way God has taken in face of such issues.

In answer to the complaint raised in Babylon over shared family guilt, God sent his word by Ezekiel the prophet that in his final disposal of human affairs, no innocent person would be punished, for the sin of another: "What do you mean by repeating this proverb... 'The fathers have eaten sour grapes,

and the children's teeth are set on edge?' As I live, says the
Lord God, this proverb shall no more be used by you in Israel.
Behold, all souls are mine; the soul of the father as well as the
soul of the son is mine; the soul that sins shall die" (Ezek 18:
2–4).

Moreover, by another great prophet he taught that the
answer he was going to give to 'tragedy in solidarity' was going
to be 'salvation in solidarity' He was going to give this family
solidarity which is the cause of so much suffering and tragedy,
a redemptive purpose. In one of his poems about a Suffering
Servant of God (in Isaiah 53) he draws a picture of how, within
this tragic transfer of sin and guilt to each other within family
and community life, an innocent one can suffer not only
because of the sin of others around him but also on behalf of
others around him. He pictures one uniquely sinless individual
living his perfect life out in the midst of many who are so
heedless of God's love, that they all live lives completely alien
to his will. Because of Their hatred of God they hate and
persecute the one who serves him and eventually kill him. But
then after his death a strange transformation takes place. They
are led to repentance. The memory of the innocence of the
one they have martyred begins to haunt them and change
them, and the thought of his patient sinless love leads them to
repentance and new life. Then they begin to understand the
reason why this innocent man suffered so much. God had
actually been working in their midst transferring their own
sins and their guilt to this innocent one and pardoning them
because his innocent servant 'bore the sin of many and made
intercession for the transgressors' (Isa 53:12). Are we not meant
to marvel and to be grateful, that God, even at the time when
such darkness was depressing the minds of men and women,
was beginning to open up new avenues of thought that were
drawing their minds towards a better future and enabling them
to live with real hope in what was to come?

Points for Further Thought and Discussion

The word of the prophet at Bethel was confirmed by several striking miracles. (The shattering of the altar, the withering of the hand, and finally by the behaviour of the lion!). Does God ever resort to such events today to confirm the truth of his Word? What does the New Testament suggest to us on this question?

What are the circumstances in which it is still inappropriate for the Church to accept gifts – even for charitable purposes?

Can you see any meaning for ourselves in our Christian work today in the prophet's being forbidden not to delay or turn back or have fellowship with any person on his mission cf. e.g. Luke 10:4, Phil 3:13–14.

Think of ways in which the accusation that we have 'thrust God behind our backs' could be applied to attitudes prevalent in our world today. Are we ourselves in danger?

Notice the searching question put to Jeroboam's wife by Ahijah – in 14:6. List particular ways in which we ourselves tend to become guilty of such pretence.

Think of ways in which we ourselves within the solidarity of community life can 'bear one anothers burdens, and so fulfil the law of Christ' (Gal. 6:2).

Notes

Man of God
Moses and David are both referred to as being a 'man of God' and in early times the title was given to a few of the prophets such as Elijah and Elisha who were regarded as especially close to God, above the usual level of those who were simply 'prophets' (cf,. Amos 7:14). A feature of the man of God was that his words came true (1 Kings 17:24)

The Factual Difficulties in this Chapter
Commentators, often find difficulty in accepting that the stories
of this chapter can have a solid historical basis. Chief among
the offensive elements is the difficulty in believing that a word
spoken at the time of Jeroboam could refer, in the specific
and detailed way occurring here, to an event which was to take
place three hundred and fifty years in the future, naming even
the king (Josiah) who would then reign in Judah, or naming
already the city of Samaria which was not then founded. This
difficulty is explained by maintaining that this story arose from
some local tradition preserved around the shrine of Bethel
which was fitted into an incident which occurred when the
shrine there was actually destroyed in the time of Josiah, the
story finding then its final form. There are also difficulties
about the frequent recurrence of the miraculous element,
especially in the extraordinary story of the rival prophet, the
lion and the donkey which one commentator lists amongst
the strangest of the Old Testament.

   We will continue to face many such miracle stories when we
come to the ministry of Elijah and we begin to deal with this
specific problem in an article (see p.115) under that heading.
We ourselves see no objection to the supposition that the story
about the altar at Bethel could have been elaborated at the
place after the incident, and brought up to date before it was
included in the King's narrative. We see no point, however, in
dismissing the extraordinarily subtle story of the two prophets
as merely fantastic legend. Granting the element of miracle, it
is too profound in this setting and true to life to be discussed
in such a way, and it illuminates in an important way the career
of Jeroboam.

CHAPTER X

TALES OF TWO KINGDOMS
1 Kings 14: 21 – 16: 34

The Narrative

We are given here a survey, first of what happened in
Judah from the latter days of Rehoboam on through the
next two reigns, then what happened in Israel during
almost the same period. The trend of events differs. In
both realms the people tend to embrace the local Baal
religion and worship at the 'high places'. In Judah political
stability is given by the appearance of God-fearing kings
who tend to bring people back to faith. In Israel, however,
after a series of disorderly revolutions, many years of
orderly rule are ensured by the appearance of a strong
dictator. He and his successors are sworn devotees of Baal.
We are to find that God is well prepared to meet this
establishment of paganism. He is now going to prove how
decisively his word can triumph over false religion.

The Kings of Judah – Hope amidst Decline

In the account of the reign of Rehoboam the reader is given a
few details of what are called the *'abominations of the nations,
which the Lord drove out before the people of Israel'* (14:24). These
were indulged in at *'high places'* – local shrines here and there
all over the land, often on hill tops, and devoted to the worship
of Canaanite deities, especially to Baal, the local divine 'Lord',
who was regarded as owning the whole locality, and was
responsible for the fertility of the land. The sacred *'pillars and
Asherim...under every green tree'* (14:23) were altars or images or

97

symbols of Ashtaroth, a female goddess, who was regarded as
the consort of Baal. The '*prostitutes*' (14:24) could be male or
female attendants at the ceremonies which involved sexual
activities so that Baal could have his desired effect.

All this contrasts starkly with Israel's worship of the Lord
in Jerusalem which was described for us so nobly in the
account of the dedication of the temple. We are therefore
meant to read with astonishment and disgust that towards
the end of Solomon's own reign he himself built such shrines
for his foreign wives, and himself indulged. As true godliness
lost its hold over the community the reversal to such heathen
practices accelerated and spread. We will eventually find out
that this localised 'paganism' gradually and ultimately took
such a firm grip even in Judah, that the most zealous of
reforming kings found it impossible to cleanse the nation
from its shameful addiction, and the final cure was effected
only during the bitter experiences undergone in the exile in
Babylon.

Rehoboam's weak beginning characterised much of his
seventeen years' reign. He was unable to withstand an invasion
by Pharaoh, king of Egypt who robbed him of much of his
gold, and it may have been the influence of his mother, an
Ammonite, which made him yield to the spread of the 'high
place' idolatry which took deep root among his people. The
Book of Chronicles tells us that he made a vain effort to bring
his people to repentance (cf. 2 Chron. 12). His failure is there,
put down to the fact that 'he had not set his heart to seek the
Lord'. Abijam his son was as powerless as himself to halt the
decline of the nation. Of him the epitaph is that '*his heart was
not wholly true to the Lord*' (15:3) and he had additional difficulty
coping with a war against Israel.

Before we read of Asa we are given the hope, by a comment
of the writer, that God will always keep alive the lamp he has
lit, for David's sake, and '*establish Jerusalem*' (1 5. 4–5). This
promise seems to be our introduction to Abijam's son Asa who
'*did what was right in the eyes of the Lord*' (15:11). He showed his
zeal early, expelling the male prostitutes and even depriving
his mother of her status as queen mother because she practised
idolatry, Yet even though his heart was '*wholly true Lord all his
days*' (15:14) he did not always behave wisely and he could

lapse badly at times (see note). Perhaps this is why he was not fully able to overcome the '*high places*'.

We can discern within this first account of the succession of kings in Judah a pattern that will appear again and again. As king follows king there is a threatening tendency to corruption and decline. Yet the succession of bad kings is regularly and marvellously arrested by the appearance of a good one, and a renewal of true godliness and faith takes place at least for a while. We will find as we follow the course of events through the coming centuries that the number of good kings and bad kings are nearly equal and that the good kings tend to reign longer. As long as he is able to achieve some measure of success God does seek, for David's sake, to keep a lamp alight in Jerusalem.

The Kings of Israel – To the Rise of the House of Omri

After his preliminary sketch of kingship in Judah the writer concentrates our minds, for many chapters to come, on the history of the kingdom of Israel.

Nadab, the son of Jeroboam lasted only two years, walking '*in the way of his father*' (15:26). He was killed by Baasha the first king murderer– a blood-thirsty man who exterminated not only all sons of the house of Jeroboam who might claim the throne, but every living relative. He hated Judah and went to war against Asa. Yet his own house was condemned to destruction by a prophet sent from God. He was condemned for imitating and walking in the ways of the very man Jeroboam whose memory he had tried to obliterate, and whose house he had destroyed! He himself managed to survive for twenty years on his throne but his son Elah, indulging in drink and sloth, aroused the contempt of Zimri, one of his high officials who executed God's judgement and himself seized the throne. Zimri had only a few days rule, but that gave him time to wipe out every male relative or friend of Baasha.

As so often happens amidst such civil unrest, the army took over, and after civil war between two military factions, Omri was put in power. It did not come within the purpose of the writer of our narrative to tell us here much about Omri himself.

Yet we have to give him credit for rescuing Israel from the anarchy it could not otherwise have survived. Within a comparatively brief period he made it a power to be reckoned with among neighbouring nations like Syria and Moab which otherwise would have crushed it. He entered a strong alliance with the kingdom of Tyre. The Assyrian empire was at that time gaining world ascendancy and he won the respect of its ruler. What concerned the writer of our narrative however, was chiefly to relate two facts about him. Firstly that he bought a hill which he saw to have great potential as a site of a new city, and he built Samaria. It was strategically placed, had great economic potential, and proved in the later war to be able to withstand a long siege. Secondly, he opened up the whole of his kingdom to the influence of Baal worship.

Though the people of God had always found it a temptation, whenever they settled in the land they had conquered, to indulge in the rites of the native local Canaanite worship, such worship was generally regarded as an unworthy pursuit, belonging to the undesirable background human life. When Omri came to the throne, however, the situation completely altered. He '*did more evil than all who were before him*' (16:25). Powerful in personal influence, he not only himself indulged openly in Baal idolatry, but he made statutes giving it a legitimate place within the nation's life (Mic 6:16). Ahab, his son, after him, went to the length of marrying Jezebel, the daughter of his father's ally, the king of Tyre. He allowed her to use her position as queen to propagate her idolatry within his kingdom. Not only did she give privilege and honours to those who adopted the new religion, she also set about persecuting with relentless perseverance and cruelty those who were loyal to the old faith. Such was her influence that Ahab built a temple of Baal in Samaria, affirming Baal religion as an officially recognised alternative to the God of Israel. We are not surprised that Baal flourished in the already degenerate religious atmosphere of Israel. Not only so, it began also to threaten the religious life of Judah. In the reign of Ahab old antagonism between North and South began to break down and a friendship arose between the two kings. Ahab's daughter by Jezebel, Athaliah, was married to the son of Jehoshaphat of Judah. She was a character no less formidable than her mother, and fanatically devoted to her pagan religion.

Baal versus the Lord – The Issues at Stake

We will understand the nature and importance of struggle into
which God was now to send Elijah, the prophet, if we first of
all try to understand the issues he faced as he confronted the
situation before him.

Each of the two religions in conflict found its origin and its
continuing source of inspiration in an entirely different source
than the other,. Baal religion arose within the mystery of being
close to nature in the created world. Certainly it must have
had a feeling for what was beautiful and occasionally
comforting in the natural world, but also at the same time it
was especially inspired by wild and uncontrolled elements in
nature, by sex, and by myths of sex-orientation of its
traditionally imagined gods. Baal understood and responded
to sex because he had sex in his make-up. The religion of the
God of Israel, on the other hand had arisen for people out of
encounters and experiences within their history as a nation.
God had proved himself to be One who had chosen them from
out of all other peoples to be of special service in redeeming
mankind from its bondage to idolatry, falsehood and evil ways.
He had continually inspired them by the word he had spoken
to their leaders about a great future for themselves and all
nations, and he had continually proved the redeeming power
of that word in a marvellously unique series of events in which
they were certain he had been personally guiding and
protecting them. He was the One who had been a friend of
Abraham, Isaac, and Jacob, who had appeared to Moses at the
bush, divided the Red Sea to deliver them from slavery, and at
Sinai had entered a solemn covenant with them, and revealed
his will especially in the Ten Commandments.

It is true that when they spoke about this God to each other
they always spoke as if were a male person. They knew, however,
that in himself he was above and beyond sex. He was able in
his own glorious and unique way to enjoy what we on our level
know as 'fellowship', but he did not require or want another,
supplementary and opposite to himself, to give him any kind
of self-expression or satisfaction or creativity. They thought of
him as creating the world, the heaven and the earth, out of
nothing, by speaking his word 'Let there be…' The natural

world was given to man to be lived in, and enjoyed, to give evidence of his love and power, but not to be made a central source of our religious ecstasy. Sex was what he had marvellously made to belong to the earthly creation, as a means of fellowship and procreation to be used and enjoyed according to his law.

The two religions contrasted not only in their views of the nature of God, and how to approach him, but also in their views of the kind of response and service he inspired in, and sought from, his worshippers. The God of Israel was characterised by holiness, mercy and faithfulness and demanded that worshippers should reflect in their dealings with each other the same mercy and faithfulness. In dealing with him, men and women were often deeply disturbed in conscience and acutely felt the need to have sin dealt with through atonement and forgiveness. To follow and serve him brought people into tension with themselves, and the accepted ways of the surrounding world. It demanded lives of discipline and self-denial. It was easy, on the other hand, to give themselves up wholly in devotion to Baal. He stimulated the erotic love that finds pleasure in self-satisfaction. His generative power was indeed stimulated by rites that included sex. He could be influenced especially by the ecstasy aroused in the rhythm and music of the dance.

People felt 'at home' with Baal religion. They felt they had it in their nature to follow such a cult. This is why Israel easily lapsed into it when they lost hold of the love and power of the Lord and had grown weary of his service. This is why Elijah's task was so difficult. The reader should recognise at this point in our story that what was at stake was so important that the long term purpose of Israel's history could not have been fulfilled without Elijah achieving success. Yet it was quite impossible for any individual or group of followers to achieve such success by the force of merely human persuasion, and the natural resources at their disposal. Therefore in this coming period in Israel's unique history, as occasionally at other decisive periods, God sealed their human witness more often than at other periods, with miraculous signs. This is why the reader is now entering a section of the history unusually full of the miraculous element. (see note p.115).

The Long-drawn-out Conflict

With the rise of the House of Omri we therefore come to a critical point in the history of the whole of Israel (both North and South) as the people of God. The Baalism which Jezebel imported from Tyre was of a form completely antagonistic to what was precious and important in the tradition that had been revealed to them in the Word of God as it had come to them throughout their past history.

God had to take decisive action. Here was a serious challenge to his direction and control of the affairs and destiny of his people. His reputation among the surrounding nations was also at stake. Moreover, many of his sincere people, like Elijah the Tishbite in perplexity and anger were praying to him to deliver his people from this curse.

It is a remarkable feature of the Book of Kings that suddenly here at the end of the sixteenth chapter the speed with which we have been moving through history of both kingdoms slows down and the next seventeen chapters are taken up with very detailed account of events which occur mainly in North Israel during more than one generation. God obviously regarded the threat posed by Baal religion was so serious that it required a decisive and quite distinct answer. He met its challenge in a whole series of historical events always dramatic and often marvellous, dominated by the work and witness of the prophets, Elijah and Elisha. He revealed the emptiness of the promises of the invading paganism and the deceptiveness of its charm. He broke its power and destroyed its influence. Indeed, he lavished on this small section of his kingdom during this brief period a wealth of self revealing activity which proved to them beyond all doubt that he had lost nothing of the power he had shown to their fathers when he led them out of Egypt and through the wilderness. He also struck many fresh notes which were meant to enrich their understanding of himself, and of the way he was going to lead them into their future. We have, for instance, in these forthcoming chapters not only spectacular public manifestations of the power of his word, but also a fascinating series of often marvellous little incidents which enrich our understanding of how his love and power work within the daily lives of ordinary people. These serve much the same purpose as the miracles Jesus did within his own ministry. They take place here and there, often in quite secluded circumstances. They were meant to bring home to his people in a quite new way how much he cared for them in poverty, sickness, in urgent domestic situations, and of how near his goodness and his kingdom, with all its power, can be to those who hear and trust in his word.

Of course those who witnessed and understood what happened during these very decisive years treasured their memories of it. Their stories were preserved especially within the schools of the prophets which flourished at the time and finally were given their due place in Holy Scripture. The importance of Elijah as one of the greatest leaders Israel ever had, is recognised in the prominent place he is given in the New Testament. Jesus himself had no hesitation in following, in his own miraculous work, the pattern of some of Elisha's miracles. These stories will prove themselves relevant in the continuing struggle that will take place in every age of the Church between truth and error, between the Gospel and its perverse forms.

Points for Further Thought and Discussion

Compare the comment on Abijam in 15:3 and on Asa in 15:14 – yet even Asa kept something back! What does this say about the Church today and about ourselves?

Read 15: 4–5 State in up-to-date terms the hope that this holds out for the future of the Church today, and the assurance we can draw from it.

What was it about David, do you think, that gave God such pleasure and confidence as he looked back over his life.

During its history, Judah was kept more stable than Israel because God now and then gave them leaders who pleased him. Even an occasional good leader saved the nation from corruption. Jesus said to his disciples, 'You are the salt of the earth'. What are the implications for us as Christians, and as a Church, today?

When Jesus said, 'You cannot serve God and mammon' he was warning that the pursuit of wealth and power could become a religion, replacing God in their lives. Has the pursuit of uncontrolled sex become as powerful a factor in our life today?

Notes

Asa in the Book of Chronicles
The book of Chronicles in three fascinating chapters gives us some illuminating information on Asa. It informs us that at the height of his reforming career, having repaired the altar at Jerusalem, he led the whole people in a religious renewal accompanied by great sacrifice to enter a covenant to rededicate themselves to God. All this was in response to a marvellous answer to prayer in a battle against overwhelming odds (2 Chron. 14–15). Yet it also underlines the degeneration that marked the latter part of his life. He failed to trust God when he was attacked by Baasha. In his fear he bought the support of the king of Damascus by raiding the treasury of the

Temple, imprisoned the prophet Hanani who rebuked him
and inflicted cruelties on those who politically opposed him
(2 Chron. 16).

The Rebuilding of Jericho

After Jericho was destroyed, by means of a miraculous
intervention by God, Joshua solemnly uttered a curse on
anyone who would attempt to rebuild it (Josh. 6:26). Some
suggest that the complex wording of this passage means that
Hiel, of Bethel, was so deeply influenced by Canaanite belief
in the efficacy of child sacrifice that he deliberately offered up
his sons, one at the beginning and the other at the completion,
of his plan for Jericho. But his sons, possibly, simply died in
the course of the re-building and their death was regarded as
the fulfilment of the prophecy. The rebuilding of Jericho was
strategically important for the defence of the now growing
realm of the house of Omri under Ahab.

CHAPTER XI

ELIJAH AND THE FAMINE
I Kings 17

The Narrative

The prosperous Baal regime in Israel under Ahab and Jezebel is suddenly disturbed by the appearance of the prophet Elijah with his condemnation of idolatry, and his announcement of the coming famine. Elijah, in danger of his life, is protected and sustained miraculously first at the brook Cherith, and then in the home of a widow at Zarephath. In a series of significant events he is tested, encouraged, and trained for the struggle he will have to face in his future public encounters with the authorities and people in Israel.

A Declaration of War

Elijah's mission was to expose the falsity of Baal religion and to begin the ruthless and bitter conflict that was in the long term to bring about the downfall of the house of Omri and of Jezebel. His aim was to make it impossible for any succeeding generation of God's people ever again to turn back to such idolatry. His first task was to reveal the sheer incompatibility of trying to serve both the Lord and Baal

His proclamation: '*There will be neither dew nor rain in the next few years except at my word*' (v. 1 N.I.V.) was like a declaration of war on the whole set-up in Israel. It will prepare the way immediately for the decisive conflict between himself and the pagan priests at Carmel, and it will set in motion the course

that the history of both Israel and Judah will take during the
next two generations.

When, later, prophets such as Isaiah or Jeremiah introduced
themselves to their people, they based their authority to be
heard on a dramatic encounter with God, accompanied by a
vision (cf. Isaiah 6:1ff.; Jer. 1:4–10). Elijah, when he introduced
himself in his day did not speak of any such experience in
order to justify his claim to be a prophet. Yet he did claim to
have been given personally a quite unique status before God.
(cf. 17:1 *Before whom I stand* A.V., R.S.V.). In this stage of his
ministry he is so near to God and so continually sensitive to
what he says, that every significant movement he makes is
prefaced by a command from God telling him to do exactly
what he does. (cf. vv. 3, 9; 18:1).

Elijah understood perfectly the prevailing religious mood
of the people, and their way of thinking. Not for years had any
of them heard the kind of word or seen the kind of vision that
had been the inspiration of the religion of their fathers. And
they had steadfastly themselves refused to heed or seek God
and go his way. They now viewed him as dead! Irrelevant! He
belonged to the past, to the desert in which he had been
conceived. They, themselves, had moved on and were now in
Canaan and in the Post-Sinai era of their nation's life – a
liberated generation! They had given themselves up to become
feverishly gripped by Baal religion – the divine in man and
woman and nature! How thankful they were that the old
restraints and disciplines that had so cramped their personal
life had lost their clammy power! The prophets word was here
pointed and direct – warning and good news together: 'He lives!'

Because so little was known about Elijah and he had such
poor credentials, no doubt at first, when he spoke of a coming
famine and called for repentance some must have thought
him crazy. It was gradually, as time passed, and a famine really
began to hurt them, that they found themselves beginning to
heed. Questions arose. The Ahab-Jezebel regime had been one
of plenty and prosperity – and now, quite suddenly, poverty!
Baal, they had been told, controlled the rain, and zeal in his
worship would certainly bring fertility – and now, at a word
from the Lord God of their fathers, he seemed to have lost his
potency! They were inclined to think again. Did the Lord still

live? Was this drought really his judgement and was he ready
to have mercy? No such thoughts troubled Ahab, at first only
hatred. His special agents were sent to every kingdom and
nation to kill Elijah wherever they could find him.

In the New Testament, James gives us important insight into
what prompted Elijah to make his initial challenge to his
generation and enter this crucial ministry (James 5: 17–18).
The famine, we are told, was brought about by his earnest
prayer. He was a very ordinary person who under the
inspiration of God's spirit allowed himself to become deeply
ashamed, burdened, and grieved over the tragic blindness to
truth, and the cheapness of life that prevailed everywhere, and
knowing God's goodness and mercy, he felt personally
responsible for bringing about change in the most effective
way he knew. His ministry therefore began with intercession –
this wonderful weaving together of anxious human
commitment of heart, with sovereign divine will, that has time
and again been the beginning of radical change in the whole
human situation.

Elijah in Hiding

The series of marvellous little stories with which our chapter
continues to unfold can bring us the assurance that God will
not fail to be especially watchful over, and concerned for, the
practical needs of those whom he engages in his service, so
that in all things God works for good to those who love him
(Romans 8:28). When Jesus sent out his disciples 'without
purse, bag or sandals' they lacked nothing (Luke 22:35). Elijah
is for a while tantalisingly and securely protected under the
very nose of Ahab who is seeking him, alive or dead, all over
the earth. And he is fed. Some scholars wishing to minimise
the supernatural element point out that the Hebrew word
translated 'ravens' is almost identical to the word 'Arabs', and
they suggest that there has been a mis-spelling of the text.
Others with the same intention suggest that the ravens brought
him scraps of carrion from the large numbers of dead animals
lying around. It seems better to accept that this is simply a
minor incident in a series of marvellous similar miracles, from

the manna in the desert to the feeding of the five thousand, and the resurrection of Jesus, which mark the course of God's path through history in working out our redemption.

Elijah's being fed by the widow-woman was equally marvellous. This passage came to Jesus' mind when he was preaching in the synagogue of his own home town. Elijah had in his day been placed exactly as he himself was, lonely and rejected by his own people, and was led by God to find help from the love and care of one who was entirely a stranger (Luke 4: 24–26)! A girl who has given up a promising career to engage in training for service in cross-cultural mission and evangelism, wrote recently to her prayer-partners of how the challenge Elijah gave to the woman to share her last meal with him, and the subsequent miracle, had all come home to her: 'I don't have much energy, time, love, patience, emotional capacity, or finances left, yet I am put in a situation that demand the very things I'm running low on. All I can do is to just let God take over. He uses the little I'm left with, and blesses the feeble effort.' These stories with their fascinating detail, have always powerfully appealed to the preacher or teacher who is willing to allow the imagination to derive such practical, allegorical, or spiritual lessons from them. A senior colleague of mine, a well known Glasgow preacher often in his pulpit referred to the important message that the text *after a while the brook dried up* (v.7) had as a solemn warning from God to his affluent, settled, and contented congregations.

Elijah in Training

In the midst of such wealth of meaning, however, we find it illuminating also to take a historical and literal approach, and to regard what happened to Elijah both at Cherith and Zarephath as designed to put him in training so that he would be more able to face the task that was to lie ahead of him in life. He was now involved himself, like Moses and Samuel before him, in the leadership of God's people. He will therefore have to become used to loneliness and rejection. He will have to be prepared for the coming experience of facing the nation with the feeling and belief that no one else around him knows, or understands, or cares for what to him are matters of life or death. His sense of utter isolation at the peak of his career will become such an insupportable burden that God will have to send an angel to give support before he makes the next lonely move. Elijah was later given an Elisha to attend him, but his main work was always accomplished pioneering alone. Here at Cherith he is being trained in the apartness that is to be such a characteristic of his future life, hardened like a nursery plant.

When he was inured to isolation, he was driven into fellowship. Away in the cities and villages of Israel men, women and children were deprived of food and water. Out in the fields in their misery and anxiety they were scraping the hard and barren earth with little reward. Some were facing death. A feature of all effective leadership in the Old Testament is always its sympathy with, and understanding of, those who were called to follow. Moreover such sympathy with those who are led is always expressed in continual and fervent intercessory prayer on the part of the leader, who has usually to pray alone. God made sure that, even in his apartness, Elijah the future leader was brought into the closest contact with the suffering and feelings of those he had been sent by God to serve and pray for, and whose existence had been so bitterly affected by the word he had spoken. When the brook dried, the command came, '*Go to Zarephath*' and there in the home of the widow along with her son, possibly in a neighbourhood where others were affected by hunger and its wasting effects, he had to live within community

He was brought most fully and effectively into training for his future leadership during the kind of experience dwelt on here by our narrator. It was a shattering experience of despair and helplessness before God. The son of the widow died, and she turned on the prophet with dismay, anger, and cynical reproach: Had not all the so-called blessing he had brought into her home, only been a preparation for calculated and cruel mockery? Why had God sent him '*to remind me of my sin and kill my son?*' (v. 18, N.I.V.) Elijah had come through much in the way of trial, danger and disappointment in the service of God, but never had he imagined himself faced with such a situation, and he was indeed shaken. The suddenness of the event, and the bitterness of the accusation shocked him. He found himself humiliated, with no possible answer and not even a word of assurance or comfort for the distracted woman. Providence had never dealt with him before in a way such as this, and what did all the previous signs of God's goodness to him mean now in face of this? He found he shared the very confusion of the woman herself. Here was the great prophet, destined to cure the woes of his nation, now floundering in face of a simple woman's pastoral situation with nothing to give her unless God himself gave it to him there and then (cf. Luke 11:6). He found himself forced to resort to prayer, alone, behind closed doors. It was a prayer of utter importunate need, demanding the whole intensity of his mind and heart. He shared with God the desperation he had shared with her, and echoed to God her complaint and argument. Soon he found himself pleading for what up till then he had believed to be impossible, and he discovered for himself, in his own experience, for the first time, the truth reiterated and rediscovered again and again at the most critical times in Israel's history – that with God 'nothing is impossible' (cf. e.g. Gen. 18:14; Jer. 32:17; Luke 1:37).

Elijah's way through Carmel and Horeb into the leadership he assumed among the prophets, will involve him in a series of situations where the obstacles are much broader, bigger, and more political than he faced in that widow's homestead, but he has now been well enough trained to be able to say even to such mountains: 'Be taken up and cast into the sea' (cf. Mark 11:23). How much that is meaningful and purposeful for life in the world can happen through acute problems that arise time and again within the confines of ordinary Christian home life, if we will allow God to take us in hand and to teach us as he taught Elijah and the woman too. She too grew in faith: '*Now I know that you are a man of God*' (v.24).

The Sign of Renewal

J. Robinson singles out one feature of Elijah's miracle for special mention by itself and we follow his example. The text of the R.S.V. we are following translates the Hebrew version of the original text. It tells us that '*Elijah stretched himself three times upon the child'*, and in his prayer, pled, '*O Lord my God, let this child's soul come into him again*' (v.21). The New English Bible translation prefers in this place to follow the original text in its Greek version which tells us that "*Elijah 'breathed deeply upon the child three times and called on the Lord, 'O Lord my God, let the breath of life, I pray, return to the body of this child'*." The commentator suggests that 'the purpose of the editors of the book of Kings in including this story was to point to Elijah's vocation as God's man, to breathe new life into God's child, Israel, who was fast becoming spiritually lifeless.' The story thus gives us the message that it was the Lord God of Israel, and not Baal who could alone give life where there was death and bring about national renewal, and it draws for us a vivid picture of the effect of the whole future ministry of this great prophet.

This is certainly a valid and fruitful line of interpretation. We, ourselves, would first of all read the incident as a literal report of a happening. Elijah, driven by an agonizing sympathy into desperate prayer, was seeking to identify himself even physically with the child so that he could take on himself the curse and the disease that were destroying his little frame, and breathe into him his own life and health. Yet the symbolic reference suggested by the above comment may also have been in the mind of the prophet himself as he responded to his whole life situation. Faced by the challenge of what seemed an impossible task, he was deliberately dedicating himself to the service of the Lord in a way that was henceforth to be typical of everything he did. Here was now to be his mission in life: to give himself as a willing sacrifice in whatever task God called him to face, however seemingly impossible. He was seeking to identify himself with the people around him in the death which seemed to have taken hold of them. He was seeking to share with them what he had been given by God to impart – life, hope and vision. The final miracle was a sign of God's acceptance of his acted prayer and self-dedication.

At whatever stage in life we happen to be, whatever the sphere of influence before us, can we not feel the constraint of this for our total self-giving to the work God has set before us?

Our thoughts can easily move from Elijah in that room to Jesus faced by Lazarus who has already lain several days in the tomb. How was it that his word had such power so that this last sign was the greatest of all he ever gave? Was it not that his prayer for it to happen was uttered out of deep self-identification with the whole tragic human situation he saw then so clearly and vividly around him. He himself at that time 'wept', and was 'deeply moved in spirit and troubled' (John 11:33). When he came to the tomb he was 'groaning within himself' (v.38, A.V.) in an agony that seemed to be the beginning of what was to be fully expressed at Gethsemone? We do not wonder that the early fathers, when they read this story of Elijah and the child, saw in it a sign of how Christ on the Cross made with us what the Reformers called the 'wonderful exchange', taking on himself from us our death, corruption and guilt, and giving us instead everything that had made his own life perfectly pleasing to the Father.

Points for Further Thought and Discussion

When God speaks his Word, what he commands happens (cf. Ps. 33:9). Here, when Elijah spoke, his word, too, had the same power as a Word of God. When we have the Bible read or preached in church we say, "Hear the Word of God", do we expect anything to happen? If so what kind of thing?

A recent writer on this chapter likened Elijah's experiences at Cherith and Zarephath to two aspects of the Christian life – its hidden apartness (cf. Col. 3:1–3) and its solidarity with life and its suffering. Is this apt? If so, in what ways do we fail to live up to it?

When God wanted to sustain and encourage Elijah he sent him to the door of a helpless and foreign stranger who seemed to have herself no means of helping him. What does this indicate about the way God means us to live today?

When he faced the critical situation that occurred in the home life he shared, Elijah was being prepared and trained for a future public ministry. Did you yourself learn important things this way? What does this suggest to parents, and the church, about the nurture of children in the home?

When the child died, Elijah was driven to prayer through anger and perplexity over the mystery of what had happened, and he did not desist till God had put things right. Read Luke 18:1–8. Can we learn from this?

Notes

On the Occurrence, Nature and Purpose of Miracles
The whole of the Old Testament is the unique history of a people to whom God, all powerful in love and goodness, has come close, so that he can deliver them from every form of evil. He is always at work in their midst shaping their history through his word, to fulfil his purposes. He works providentially and often unobtrusively within the ordinary routine of their

family and national life, forgiving and training them to pray, and answering their prayers. Yet all that he accomplishes in this long drawn out process over centuries in the realm of thought and the formation of human character, and truly oriented devotion to himself is miraculous. As Wheeler Robinson once said, 'The supreme miracle of the Old Testament is the historical development of the religion of Israel.'

Since God is so graciously near to Israel in the midst of this unique salvation history, so close in his presence, so great in his power, so pledged to overcome all evil, so strong in his purpose, it need cause us neither surprise or offence to find taking place at times, these outstanding events, which we call 'miracles', e.g. the crossing of the Red Sea. The possibility for such things to happen is there in the background of the whole historical development. Calvin notes at one point in his commentary on the Psalms that there is mention of God's 'wondrous deeds' − 'these signal and memorable benefits' − he calls them, 'in which God has exhibited a bright and shining manifestation of divine power.' 'God,' he says, 'is the author of all blessings, but some have specially evident marks' (on Psalm 9:1). Though all God's works, as viewed in the Old Testament perspective, are wonderful, yet at particular points of time and space (to cite Wheeler Robinson again) 'the wonder of what is happening is intensified.' 'A miracle' says Dibelius, is an event in which the hand of God, which is always there, can be more clearly traced than at other times.' Miracles dramatically reveal an activity which is continually taking place.

When we regard miracles in this light it is notable that God is so sparing in his use of them in the Old Testament. They occur mostly in clusters at two critical periods in the history − during the period of the Exodus and wilderness wanderings, and during the period we are now entering when Israel's faith was under its most serious threat from falsehood and Baalism. Calvin notes that the extraordinary miracles of God happen where and when there is a special need for them. Discussing the miracle of the rod turned into a serpent he underlines the fact that Moses, outwardly unimpressive and weak (an earthen vessel) had to be 'rendered formidable' to Pharaoh by God (Comm. on Exod. 7:10). The miracles authenticate the witness of the prophets. Moreover, through them God not only demonstrates his presence and power but also illuminates his purpose and the nature of his will and message. As one commentator puts it 'God used miracle to teach us truths about himself, his nature and purposes, which he could express in no other way'.

On Allegorical Interpretation

The reader will have noticed that on at least three occasions in the exposition of this chapter we have deliberately given an allegorical interpretation of the text (on v. 7, vv. 13–14 and v. 21). We find that occasionally, especially where there is a miraculous element, certain aspects of the narrative lend themselves to such interpretation. The word 'allegory' means 'saying something else' and to interpret a passage allegorically can at times mean finding in a passage a meaning which the human author at the time of writing might not have consciously intended.

Sometimes a writer consciously writes a deliberately allegorical work, intending that his terms or characters should have a double meaning (e.g. John Bunyan's 'Pilgrim's Progress') and there are such passages in the Bible. Literary critics point out that it is also a characteristic of some classical literature and especially modern literature that its author conveys sometimes unconsciously and sometimes with vague and fugitive intention a deeper meaning than lies on the surface of the work. Language, too, is such that often a phrase can carry a double meaning. The Bible, too, has occasionally such characteristics deliberately appealing often to the human imagination as we read it. The miracle stories of Jesus, for example, make it obvious that at times he had dual purpose in what he did. As long as we stress the fact that we are reading history where history is intended, and try to seek and respect the intention of the author, we need not be so over-cautious as to exclude such helpful allegorical interpretations as occasionally offer themselves.

CHAPTER XII

THE SHOW-DOWN AT CARMEL
I Kings 18

The Narrative

Elijah, in hiding, hears the call finally to face Ahab and to challenge him and the priests of Baal to a contest on Mount Carmel. At Carmel there took place one of the most decisive and dramatic events in Israel's history. The Word of God spoken by Elijah was completely vindicated and the emptiness and futility of Baal worship were fully exposed. As we watch Elijah enter the public arena to issue his challenge, we marvel both at his courage and at the compliance of Ahab to his plan.

Elijah Shows Himself

Elijah felt he had been called by God to play the part of a second Moses in the history of Israel. Israel had rejected God's covenant, broken down his altars and was prepared to slay all his prophets (cf. 19: 14). He believed he had been sent not only to rebuild what had been broken, but to bring about the rebirth of the nation. In his prayer at the altar at Carmel he expresses what he believed God was going to do through him: '*That this people may know that thou, O Lord, art God, and that thou hast turned their hearts back*' (v. 37)

We are certainly meant to marvel at the descent of the fire and the coming of the rain which Elijah prayed for on the top of Carmel. Just as marvellous, however, was the courage given to him to go out immediately God said 'go', in simple and confident faith, to attempt what must have seemed an

118

impossible task. The greatest miracle of all is to be seen in the authority with which he took command of the whole daunting situation from moment to moment without a trace of hesitation, his sustained calm resolve, and the physical and nervous power given to him to see everything through till he had fully won the day for God. Among all the great events in Israel's history, what he did matches in its sheer boldness and determination what Moses did when he went from the desert to Pharaoh and demanded the freedom of God's people, and what David did when he faced Goliath. What makes his achievement all the greater is that he was naturally of a temperament far more vulnerable and nervous than were either Moses or David. The prominent place given to him in the New Testament is a tribute to his influence on the whole subsequent history and tradition of Israel.

We can imagine his questioning and his fears as he set out. The outline of the task must already have been clear in his mind. God had promised rain, but before it came he had to contact the king, to demand a national assembly and a public contest between himself and the priests of Baal on the summit of Carmel. Perhaps he had gone over some of the details of what he would say to Ahab in making his challenge, but he was not one to prepare set speeches. The questions and doubts must have piled up in his mind. How was he going to persuade Ahab to agree, and what if he did not agree? What protection would he find anywhere? What would he say if finally he did stand face to face with a whole people bitter over the death of their children and cattle? Who would stand by his side and help him to repair the altar and make the sacrifice? The first stage of the journey through parched countryside and desolate homesteads cannot have been propitious. His encounter with Obadiah must have been daunting. He heard from him how Jezebel in her rage had slaughtered many of his friends, and he discovered that this man of God, from whom he had expected some support, could not, by this time, perfectly trust him (vv. 9–14).

A change began however when he met Ahab. The king in anger threw at him the accusation that it was he, with his attempt to bring back to Israel his antiquated religious belief, who had incurred the wrath of Baal and caused the misery that had struck the nation, '*You troubler of Israel*' (v.17). Elijah, equally in anger at the utter falsehood, and with extraordinary boldness turned the accusation back squarely on the king himself '*I have not troubled Israel, but you have and your father's house*' (v.18). A devastating public indictment against the royal house followed, and strangely, Ahab had not the courage to utter even a threat. We are reminded of how Moses suddenly received the power from God to command the seas to divide and to persuade a bewildered people to follow him into the gulf (cf. Ex. 14:17–21). For a few brief hours every word Elijah utters seems to take on the power of a word coming from God himself. He makes no false step. None can withstand what he commands. Even stubborn and hitherto revengeful Ahab has obediently to order the gathering that is eventually to bring about his downfall. The people of Israel gather as he calls them, prepared to listen as if he had their whole future in his hands.

The Call to Face the Truth

On the mountain Elijah did not need to say much to the common people in condemnation of their folly and sin. It soon became obvious that the years of famine had already been an adequate sign of the anger and judgement of God. Most of them were perplexed and disillusioned. Their resistance to God had been partially broken. Elijah's task, like that of Samuel at an earlier crisis in their history (1 Sam. 7:3) was to issue a call, as simply and directly as he could, to turn back now to the Lord their God and forsake their idolatry. He made it clear that their decision had to be not only about which God they were going to prefer to worship, but about which way of life from now on they were going to follow. '*How long will you go limping with two different opinions? If the Lord is God, follow him; but if Baal then follow him*' (v. 21) – two paths ahead, each in an opposite direction – two incompatible ways of life, standards of values, and sets of laws – two opposing cultures and destinies! It was not a case of simply giving up the orgies on the 'high places' but of returning with all seriousness of purpose to the covenanted way of life, to the laws that had made their fathers unique before God – 'a kingdom of priests, and a holy nation' (Ex. 19: 5–6).

His appeal obviously re-echoes the first of the Ten Commandments, 'You shall have no other gods before me' (Deut. 5:7). We hear this command especially in its exclusive form : 'The Lord is God in heaven above and on the earth beneath. There is no other ' (Deut 4:39). Nothing must even be mentioned alongside of him, when the basis, aims, and hope of our life are in question. We cannot have two masters (Mt. 6:24). No way of life not centred on him alone, can bring any satisfaction or faithfulness. No worship directed otherwise than to him alone can have any reality or truth. We have the commandment also in its more totalitarian from: 'Love the Lord your God with all your heart and with all your soul, and with all your might' (Deut. 6:4). Whatever honour or deference we seek to pay to him means nothing, if at the same time we place in our loyalty and affection something else alongside of him.

In pursuing his appeal he resorted to ridicule. The mockery in his tone and language is well conveyed by translation that asks, *'How long will you go hopping lamely between two opinions?'* It is as if he were drawing a cartoon of their behaviour to bring out its sheer stupidity. Some commentators think that he is referring to the fact that in their dances in Baal worship they bent themselves in a low squatting position. The way people take when they forsake God is always absurd. No one ever brought this out more powerfully than Jesus with his word-pictures of the self-deluded multitudes, by-passing the narrow way of life and thronging the broad way to destruction, and of the builders devoting all their skill, and the toil of a whole life time, to build a fine house on sinking sand. (Mt. 7:13, 24–27). Jesus was here following the great prophets who so frequently ridiculed the behaviour of those around them in the practices of their idolatry (Jer. 2:13; Isa. 44:12–20; 46:1–2). Perhaps it was Elijah who here sets the pattern for such a powerful means of appeal. It is indeed a sign of how confident he felt in his own case that he could take this approach. He was soon to use this same weapon of ridicule with devastating effect in his show-down with the priests of Baal.

When he says *'how long?'* he was touching a sensitive spot in the present experience of his hearers, to make an evangelistic

appeal. They had thought it a step of courage when they broke
with their past and adopted the Baal way of life. It had seemed
to promise luxuriant breadth of experience, the fuller life that
they as human being's were made for. But now, to many of
them, the famine in the land was a reflection of the inward
need of their hearts and minds. They were disillusioned and
weary. Life had lost not only the stability and purpose which
had once belonged to them as a people, but even its natural
freshness and sweetness, – and even before Elijah asked the
question they were themselves wondering 'how long' it need
go on? In his very raising of this question Elijah was preaching
good news. They need wait no longer! Everything can change
here and now, and God has sent him to tell them so!

The Contest

Sometimes God used human eloquence alone to move his
people to respond to him (cf. Josh. 24:24; Neh. 8:1–12). Here
on Carmel in response to Elijah's appeal, the people said
nothing (v. 21). Elijah had therefore now to prepare for the
contest and the miracle (cf. 1 Sam. 12: 16–20). His word had
certainly not been in vain. It had created the atmosphere in
which he could proceed to set the stage for the miracle that
was to come, and it was to give direction and spontaneity to
their response when it occurred.

In seeking to understand the inspiration received by Elijah
on Mount Carmel we have to remember that the prophets of
Israel were a quite uniquely inspired group of people doing a
special task for God within the purpose of salvation which he
was working out through the history of Israel. Though by
nature they were men like ourselves, and had to exercise faith
within perplexing situations, nevertheless at times they 'stood
in the counsel of the Lord' (Jer. 23:18) and were privy to his
will in a way that we are not in a position to understand today
from our own experience, or even from our study of other
contemporary religions. It would be as foolish to imagine that
Elijah devised this contest and planned the miracle as it would
be to imagine that Moses planned the passage through the
Red Sea, and the defeat of Pharaoh. Elijah is not here

challenging God to do anything, it is rather God who has
planned the whole affair and is challenging Elijah to obey him.
Elijah is facing no risk that the fire might not descend from
heaven. The verse which provides an important key for our
understanding of the whole affair is in his prayer that the
people might know '*that I have done all these things at your
command*' (v. 36, N.I.V.).

His certainty about what God will do therefore inspires
everything he himself does. He is concerned for complete
openness. He calls them to draw near (v. 30) and watch his
every movement as he repairs the altar, and arranges the
sacrifice, fills the dug trench with nothing but water, and pours
deliberately again and again. He arranges it all with
consummate skill. From the beginning everything is designed
to confuse his opponents, to cause their complete humiliation,
to expose the nonentity of Baal, and to bring out the contrast
between him and the living God. One of the attributes for
which Baal was most famous was that he was a God of fire. He
is going to be shown to have no fire when he is challenged
really to prove himself. Elijah is so confident that the Lord will
be ready without delay to send *his* fire, that he is able to give
the Baal priests almost the whole day to prove their complete
impotence. He acted like the ring-master of a circus and, as if
at the crack of a whip, controlled the pace of the performance.
From morning till noon they did what was expected of them,
calling on the name of Baal, limping around the altar with
their crouching dance. Since nothing was happening he began
to taunt them. Should they not try to shout louder? Perhaps
their God was deep in thought, or busy with other affairs (some
commentators suggest that this was understood by his hearers
to suggest that he had gone to the loo') or had he gone on a
journey? – or did he need to be awakened out of sleep? His
mockery completed the undoing of the Baal devotees. Growing
more desperate they became more frenzied in their orgiastic
dancing, and in their 'ranting and raving' (as one translation
puts it), and as if to arouse some pity from their otherwise
unresponsive deity, began to slash themselves with swords and
spears till the blood ran.

The contrast was complete when, as evening was falling,
Elijah took over, and the people saw the quiet deliberation

with which he prepared his sacrifice, heard his impressively
simple pleading with a God with whom he seemed to be
intimate '*answer me, O Lord, answer me*' – Then '*the fire of the
Lord fell*' (vv. 37–8) De Vries sums it up well: 'What four hundred
and fifty Baal priests could not get Baal to do by dancing and
slashing all day, Yahweh did in a last brief moment before sunset
and he did this in response to the simple but powerful
supplication of his true servant. While Baal was away on a
journey or on business or sound asleep, Yahweh was alert and
attentive, only waiting until the impotency of Baal should be
fully demonstrated. Repeatedly the Baal prophets had cried,
'Baal hear us', but here had been no answer or voice.
Contrariwise one urgent prayer moves Yahweh into action'.

The Prayer and the Rain

We must not belittle Elijah or his achievement by holding
against him his slaughter of the priests. It was not a necessary
ingredient of the campaign designed for him by God. When
God himself worked out his purposes in history, and used
ordinary people in his service he had to take them just as they
were, and work with them in the midst of the superstitions
and hatreds that were as prevalent in those days as they are in
the world today, (this age of mass graves!). As he used them
they did not always respond as he planned, yet he did not cease
to hold on to them, to use them as his servants while he tried
to correct their faults. We have to note that in the vision soon
to be given at Horeb, Elijah is taught that God, though he
gave them a place in his purpose, did not want the ruthless
and bloody aspects of getting rid of Baal, to become associated
with a prophet who had been called to proclaim his name.
     We can continue to learn from Elijah through his concern
over the rain. He was sure it would now be sent. Even though
the sky was still clear he announced dramatically that a storm
was about to break, and Ahab, perhaps feeling he could feast
more liberally because of the good news, mounted his chariot
for his palace in Jezreel. It is a symbolic touch in the story that
Ahab '*went off to eat and drink, while Elijah went up to the top of
Carmel*' (v. 42) to watch and pray. The stability, health and

pleasantness of human life within a community, more than many of us realise, is due at times to the fact that while many are careless, unconcerned and even spendthrift, there are the few among them who are prepared to take on themselves the burden of real community responsibility and especially the burden of prayer and watching before God for his mercy and blessing.

We are meant to notice, in this incident, that even though God had already promised to send rain, and was going to do so, he nevertheless waited till Elijah prayed earnestly for it to happen. In the Bible it always seemed to be of real pleasure and value to God to do things for his people on earth, if he could first stir up people to pray for these things. He indeed found such pleasure in answering prayers that he loved even simply to give way to human praying. He even allowed himself at times to be actually pushed into complying with what his people prayed for (Gen. 18:22–33, Ex. 32: 9–10, 14, Gen. 32 : 26–30). He allows human beings to accomplish things by prayer. Elijah obviously felt that he must exert himself in his praying, and try to press God strongly to answer. When it says that '*he bowed himself down upon the earth, and put his face between his knees*' he was following a commonly accepted custom of his times. But it might also be that he was making a sign before God of what he desired to happen and was trying with great effort to make himself into the shape of a cloud. It is certain, however, that his prayer was made with the effort and passion that characterise prevailing prayer in the Bible.

Elijah of course expected an answer to his prayer. He sent his servant several times to look for the cloud, and he did not cease praying until he had the answer. He was asking God for what his people desperately needed. This is what the most effective prayer is mainly concerned with – matters of life and death, bread and water, and salvation, rather than with luxuries. Jesus reminded us that our prayers should be about such basic things, about our need for daily bread and for the Holy Spirit (Luke 11:3 and 13). Such prayers were to be made 'in his name' in response to his word, and inspired by his Spirit (John 14:14; 15:7; 16:24). He promised that such prayers would be answered and he encouraged us to look continually for the answers (Matt. 7: 7–11; 17: 20–21).

Elijah therefore worked wonders in his day not simply because he was a man caught up into a very special relationship with God, but also because he was a man who learned to pray as we ourselves can learn to pray, and who out of love could throw himself on his face and make intercession for men who were either too weary or too unbelieving or too preoccupied to pray for their own dire needs. The apostle James reminds us that the privilege of being able to win God's blessing for men through prayer is beyond none of us who will have it. 'The prayer of a righteous man has great power in its effects. Elijah was a man of like nature with ourselves and he prayed fervently that it might not rain, and for three years and six months it did not rain on the earth. Then he prayed again and the heaven gave rain, and the earth brought forth its fruit' (James 5: 16–18).

Points for Further Thought and Discussion

Elijah required, and was given great boldness to witness for God and to show himself. Jesus promised similar boldness to his future disciples (cf. Mark 13:11) and the Apostles showed it (cf. Acts 5:17ff.). Can you think of situations today when we, too, need this gift? – in order to show ourselves?

Think over the importance and role of Obadiah in this story – in high position in such a rotten administration, yet keeping his faith. Could Elijah have succeeded without Obadiah? Could Obadiah have endured without an Elijah?

Though Elijah did not devise the challenge he gave to God, nevertheless on Carmel he gave God the challenge that God wanted him to make. Is it ever right for us to challenge God to act in any way? e.g. to fulfil the promises of his word to us. Think of how this might apply in our personal and Church life. Are we at fault because we do not make the challenge?

Elijah had no hesitation in making people feel troubled and in accusing them of being responsible for the trouble they experienced. Is there a lesson here that we can learn from him?

Does Elijah's effective use of ridicule point to a weapon we might effectively use more in our preaching and teaching?

Note the contrast between Elijah's calm and confident praying for the fire and the strenuous and anxious effort he put into his prayer for rain. Are both attitudes justified, and should our praying at times reflect both?

Notes

Obadiah
It is worth while, in view of the forthcoming revelation of the '7000 who had not bowed the knee to Baal' to take time to appreciate this man Obadiah. He seems to have been a steward

in charge of the palace of Ahab, and he is here overseeing a
foraging operation to commandeer whatever fodder he can
claim from the impoverished countryside to keep the king's
war-horses alive. Yet he '*revered the Lord greatly*' and secretly
supported a hidden resistance movement, giving food and
shelter to persecuted prophets of the Lord. He lived amongst
the lust, treachery, and greed that pervaded Ahab's palace,
yet he had kept the faith. Possibly among all the other miracles
within this history we are meant to regard it also as a miracle
that he should be as he was, and that God gave him favour in
the eyes of Ahab. 'When a man's ways please the Lord, he makes
even his enemies to be at peace with him' (Prov. 16:7). We can
think of others like him, e.g. Daniel's influence on monarchs
like Nebuchadnezar, and Darius, Joseph on Pharaoh. Paul in
his epistle to the Philippians speaks of the believers that are
'of Caesar's household'.

Carmel

Mount Carmel was no doubt chosen by Elijah deliberately for
the contest. It was one long wooded mountain range over 1700
feet at its highest point in the territory of the tribe of Asher. It
possibly had sacred associations with those who worshipped
the Tyrian Baal and seems to have had a ruined altar to the
Lord. It had a spring which could have served to give Elijah
the water so scarce elsewhere.

CHAPTER XIII

THE SOUND OF A GENTLE WHISPER
1 Kings 19

The Narrative

Elijah, threatened by Jezebel, suddenly breaks down and takes flight, going beyond even the borders of Judah and praying to God to bring an end to his struggle. He is given sleep. An angel feeds him. Seeking God he goes to Horeb where God had revealed himself to Moses. God now reveals more aspects of his will and work than Elijah has, up till now, understood. The significant part of this revelation is a 'gentle whisper'.

From Carmel to Horeb

Elijah is more often remembered by the revelation given to him at Horeb than by what happened through him at Carmel. Many, indeed, who are ignorant of the story of the contest with the priests of Baal and the fire from heaven, know about the 'still small voice', and have found comfort and inspiration in the message it has brought to them. We can understand why the human religious memory shows such a bias, for the Horeb incident has a more universal appeal than the other.

We must not underrate what happened at Carmel. It was decisive. The religious and moral influence of Jezebel was discredited, and she will inevitably be rendered powerless. But, she has become strongly entrenched. It will take time and the effort of many others besides Elijah, before the word spoken by God in that one-day event has its full cleansing and reforming effect on the life of his people. Jezebel still feels

129

secure, and she is enraged. God uses her threat to drive Elijah on, and to ensure that his mind now becomes fully preoccupied with, and prepared for, the next phase in his career.

How are we to explain his mood and feeling as he began to take flight? Some commentators put it down to a natural reaction following over-elation, some to a nervous breakdown arising out of sheer exhaustion. One commentator, on this level suggests that 'Elijah exhibited symptoms of manic depression, wishing for death, together with loss of appetite, an inability to manage and excessive self pity.'

We prefer to take another possible line of explanation. On his journey to Horeb Elijah is entering a new important phase of his ministry and he is as completely under the hand of God at every point on this journey as we saw him to be at each stage of his great and dramatic journey towards Mount Carmel. But, from now on, (except, of course, at the moment of his death (cf. 2 Kings 2:11) he must learn to live out his life and to serve God on a much lower and more sober level than that to which he had been raised during his uniquely triumphal experience in his encounter with the priests of Baal and in the sudden conversion of his people. It cannot be avoided that he must experience exceptionally severe withdrawal symptoms as God releases him as gently as possible and brings him back to earth. We can think of what happened to him simply as the cost he has to pay for having been the Elijah of Carmel. He himself is not completely blameless. There has been some loss on his part of the faith and vision that have so far inspired his zeal and obedience, and sustained his courage. It is as if he is no longer so continually and clearly directed by the Word of God. His mind has become orientated too inwardly upon himself. His condition is like that of Peter when after so marvellously walking on the water, he found himself beginning to sink because he was no longer looking at Christ. It is a condition we all at times experience apart from any kind of natural nervous disorder.

The only clues we have to Elijah's thoughts on the journey south to the broom tree, are in the prayer. '*It is enough; now, O Lord, take away my life; for I am no better than my fathers.*' (v. 4) We need not interpret his death-wish as if he were 'seriously abandoning himself to the bitterness of failure' or 'envisaging the complete end of his mission.' It seems, rather to be a careless and quite natural expression of what he knows is a temporary mood. Obviously, too, in his perplexity he has been trying to come to terms with what has happened to him by comparing himself with such as Moses or David who has also reached strange low points in their experience (Ex. 32:19; 1 Sam. 27:1). His dominant thought is simply that 'all flesh is grass' (Isaiah 40:6). There is a longing here for something more stable and lasting than elated experience, even experience of success, in the service of God. Perhaps in the sweep of his triumph at Carmel he allowed himself to lose touch with God. What he longs for now is God himself. He feels that the best place at which he can regain his presence with the genuine and lasting reality will be to go to Horeb, the very place of the covenant he had tried to re-establish at Carmel, the place where Moses had seen his vision and heard the voice.

The Angel, the messenger of God, understood his thoughts, his longing, and his need for sleep and food, and helped to put things right for him to go on. He could have made the journey there in only a few days, but he lengthened it into a kind of pilgrimage lasting forty days and forty nights, because this was the duration of Moses' stay in the mountain as the revelation he was seeking came to him (Deut. 10:10).

We are meant to take note, on this journey, of a change that has come both in the way God is controlling Elijah, and in the response he himself is making to God. As he approached, and carried out his task on Carmel he was full of personal initiative, eager in the activity he offered to God, taking command of the situation before him. Now on this flight from Carmel to Horeb he is primarily submitting himself to the external and mental pressures that are over-taking him, learning, receiving and enduring suffering. He is wholly obedient to God in both stages of this great event, but in the first stage of the whole event his obedience can be called 'active'. In the second stage it is 'passive'. Jesus told Peter that during the prime of his life he had been allowed much self determination in his obedience, 'you went where you wanted'. But he added the prophecy 'when you are old you will stretch out your hands, and someone else will dress you and lead you where you do not want to go' (John 21: 18–19 N.I.V.). It was painful for Elijah to enter this

experience of becoming humiliated and broken in the service
of God, and to have to take flight before the anger of a godless
woman. He certainly did not at first understand, yet he learned
that he could give God as worthy obedience in submitting to
this failure, as he had in his previous soldiering victory. Our
thoughts at this point in the narrative turn to Jesus, the
'prophet mighty in word and deed,' who learned obedience
by the things he suffered (Heb. 5:8) and saved us by his
obedient passion as well as by his victory over all the powers of
evil. They also turn to Paul, our great example in the New
Testament way of life: "Therefore I will boast all the more gladly
about my weakness, so that Christ's power may rest on me.
That is why, for Christ's sake I delight in weaknesses, in insults,
in hardships, in persecutions, in difficulties. For when I am
weak, then I am strong" (2 Cor. 12: 9–10 N.I.V.). The Old
Testament, as a preparation for the New, is only at times a
faint foreshadowing of what is to come. Yet it continually points
in the right direction.

The Revelation

With the question; *What are you doing here Elijah?* (v. 4), God
was not seeking from him any detailed account of how he now
saw his past way of life, nor did he want him to engage in any
form of self-examination about his motivation as a prophet.
He is touching him so as to evoke a confession of his immediate
feelings and fears as he stood before him longing and hoping
to hear and know. Elijah frankly unburdened himself of the
lament and complaint that he had not yet been able to throw
off even after these forty days. Immediately God found him
ready in this way to pour out his heart, and keep nothing back,
the great theophany, the vision he had longed for, took place,
and he saw and heard. All God had wanted of him was this
openness! How near we can be to glory when we feel so far
away from it – if we will only be as open to God as he wants us
to be! How near to glory was that woman at the well when
Jesus met her, and how far from her thoughts what she was
going to hear and see – and all Jesus wanted to find within her
was openness (cf. John 4:4–29)!

The revelation was as abrupt as it was dramatic. The prophet was told to stand in the mouth of the cave to see it, but before he reached there, it came – '*a great and powerful wind... an earthquake... a fire ... and a still small voice*' the '*low murmuring sound*' (according to the N.E.B.) or '*the sound of a gentle stillness*' which brought the whole experience to its climax. Elijah felt the presence of God in the stillness so near and so real that fear and wonder came over him. Neither the whirlwind that scoured the side of the mountains, nor the earthquake that seemed to shake the foundations of the earth, not the fire that fell from the heavens, splendid and marvellous, forced Elijah to his knees in worship. These things did not convince his soul. It was the awe of the stillness that overwhelmed the man and made him cover his face as if he were afraid to look upon the glory of God.

God is teaching Elijah that he can pass by the earthquake and wind and fire, and still remain the Lord. He has the power to bring awe and conviction to the souls of men even without these vivid and spectacular signs of his omnipotence, fury and victory. Even if at times he sends earthquakes and thunderbolts to do his work, he remains the Lord in his power to manifest himself and work wonders in the human heart long after these spectacular things have subsided perhaps in failure, and there are no visible signs left of his presence among men. This God who had been with him in Tishbe when he received the call to be a prophet, who answered his prayers so spectacularly for the famine, the fire, and the rain, is now declaring that he will be with him as his way of life now changed, as the tasks become more mundane, as the answers to his prayers become more difficult to trace, as success takes longer and shows itself in quieter and more gradual ways.

Though it was a word spoken to a lonely and depressed prophet at the mouth of a desert cave, God had more than Elijah in mind when he spoke thus at Horeb after he spoke at Carmel. Sometimes, we ourselves are apt to lay too much stress on the importance of our own vigorous and showy activity in advancing the Kingdom of God. We give way to the idea that the blustering and spectacular way of doing things are more effective than ways that are less outwardly impressive. We need to remember that God does not necessarily herald the progress of his kingdom with noise, or with spectacularly successful Church efforts. It is one of the most remarkable features of the New Testament account of the Gospel that when he announced the most world-shaking and revolutionary event ever to take place, his complete victory over evil and death, he did not use a blaze of trumpets amplified over a vast and impressive congregation. The great news was, rather, communicated quietly and privately, mostly to a few people here and there, withdrawn from the world. Jesus did not attempt to put on a grand show. He did not advertise himself loudly to push his claims. Nor did he use pomp or display. Certainly he gave many marvellous signs of who he was, but he was anxious not to make these the central feature of his ministry. Rather, he wanted people to find a more convincing proof of the presence of God in the truth of his word and the love which he showed in his person. His presence with us today, which is often realised through a quietly spoken word – the still small voice! – is the only token we need that he loves and forgives us, wants to cure us of our depression, and that our labour is not in vain.

Of course Elijah was not meant to imagine at Horeb that God was now retracting from, or in any way minimising, the importance and splendour of what he had done through him already. We ourselves must remember that at Pentecost, as if to remind us of Carmel, there was the 'rush of a mighty wind from heaven' and 'tongues of fire,' and a series of remarkable apostolic miracles to help establish the Church in a way full of promise for the future. The remarkable spread of the Pentecostal Churches today is surely a sign to us that God, when he chooses, does make concessions to our human longing for visible signs of His Kingdom. Out of his mercy and kindness to us God can and does still use the spectacular. He can and does cause miraculous healings to take place from time to time. Providential events happen which make us say, 'This is the Lord's doing; it is marvellous in our eyes' (Ps. 118:23). The New Testament speaks of the Kingdom as finally breaking in upon this world in the midst of upheavals and signs that cause the whole earth to wonder and fear. It is a pity that so many of us who prefer the level and regular way, tend, in our anxiety to avoid the turbulent and ecstatic, to cut ourselves off from fellowship with others in what still can prove worthwhile and important.

The Task

When God speaks to us it sometimes takes a long time for us to understand what we have heard or seen. Though the repeated question, '*What are you doing here, Elijah?*' evoked verbally the same answer as before, Elijah evidenced in his tone and attitude that he had begun to think over what the revelation was meant to say to him.

A vision, in the Bible was often the prelude to a task which God had for the recipient. When Moses had his vision at the burning bush, it was to introduce him to the work ahead of him (Ex. 3: 7–10). When Peter was wondering what his dream about the net from heaven meant, there was a knock on the door summoning him to go where he would be helped to understand what the vision was all about (Acts 10:17). Immediately Elijah's vision ended, God outlined the task.

As we can imagine from the vision, his part in overcoming Baal was now to become much more subdued, private, and unsensational than it had hitherto been. There remained, of course, much to be done that would involve war and massacre. There was no other way possible to rid Israel and Judah of this curse. But let him never again himself try to take the sword. There were plenty of kings and bloody revolutionaries whom God was going to use! Let him encourage and call on others better fitted for that task. He also had now to seek mutual encouragement among others who could help him in his mission. There were seven thousand around him, and some were his own disciples, who had not bowed the knee to Baal! Down there in a farm at Abel-Meholah, were Shaphat and his son Elisha – one with himself in their hatred of Baalism! He was to start there by anointing Elisha to serve him in the work and succeed him as a prophet.

What now happened is described in some detail. Elisha and his father's servants at their ploughs immediately recognise the prophet. He had been a topic of their conversation. They were thankful that the rain had come to make it worth their while now to work on the ground. Elisha himself had probably been among the crowd at Carmel. What Elijah did, taking off his cloak and throwing it on the shoulders of the younger man carried its own obvious significance. Nothing is said and nothing needs to be said. He must follow Elijah, become his successor, and submit to his training. It was to mean a costly and radical change to his way of life.

The story reminds us of what suddenly happened to Moses when he was feeding his sheep (Exod. 3:1–2) and to Matthew when he was sitting in his tax office (Matt. 9:9) quite unexpectedly, in the midst of the routine of our lives, things around us are opened up – perhaps through the visit of a friend, or through a message on the radio, or through the reading of a book, especially the Bible, or through a sermon in Church. The living Christ comes and presses his claim upon us.

Elijah, characteristically brusque and lacking in pastoral understanding, left Elisha immediately perplexed. The man had gone on his way and said nothing! What was he to do? Was he himself allowed a decent good-bye to his parents, or did the call mean that he must deny the affection that bound him so closely to his home? He ran and pled with the older man at least to wait and give him the opportunity to express what was most human in his nature: '*Let me kiss my father and mother good-bye and then I will come with you.*' (v. 20, N.I.V.)

Elisha wants to retain something of his natural self. The typical full-time prophet of his day (like Elijah) presented too often in their public work the image of those who had become distant from life, forbidding in nature and monastically inclined. He himself does not feel that he should necessarily and deliberately hurt his godly parents or do violence to his naturally affectionate make-up. Later on in his work and ministering as a prophet, he always tended to be a little more human, more easily approachable, and responsive to the immediate domestic needs of ordinary people around him, than the typical 'man of God' of his day.

We must give Elijah credit for a very wise answer to his request. His word '*Go back again*' was encouragement to the younger man to be himself. He said farewell from that day to his home and his farm. But he said farewell in a way that made it a day of rejoicing rather than a day of gloom and tension, a day to be remembered rather than to be forgotten. He made a feast. Perhaps spoke of the call he had heard, and of what he felt this call would involve. He took his departure in full recognition of gratitude for what his home had made him.

Elijah had a further word for Elisha before he left him: '*What have I done to you?*' Many commentators think that this question merely reinforces what Elijah has already said: 'What does my opinion matter? Think for yourself.' This kind of advice can be helpful when given by a Christian leader to those who are becoming too dependent on him. Each of us must become responsible for making our own judgements on practical issues and moral questions.

There is, however, another possible interpretation of Elijah's words which fits better into the situation. What he said to Elisha could be translated: 'Go back, but remember what I have done to you.' In placing his prophet's mantle on Elisha's shoulders, Elijah had given a sign to the younger man that he was no longer his own. He must now listen always for God's Word. He must do what it commands, go where it orders. As a man of God, he can no longer speak his own thoughts or 'do his own thing'. He belongs, body and soul, mind and strength, to the Lord. He must remember always that the prophet's mantle, laid on his shoulders, and the claim it would continually make on his life and loyalty. Elisha immediately showed how well he understood what Elijah had said and done. In giving his farewell feast, he slew his oxen, and used the wood of their yokes as fuel to boil their flesh. The slaying of the oxen was a sign that he was sacrificing to God what was most precious in his former way of life. The destruction of the yokes was a sign that never again would he come back and take up this work.

The problem Elisha had to face can often occur today. Any deep and sudden religious experience can be disturbing. It was a wise teacher who advised his students for the ministry to exercise great toleration and pastoral understanding towards the over-enthusiastic behaviour of people who have undergone a radical conversion since, as he put it 'they sometimes have to be made human again, and it can take a year or two.' It is a pity that needless grief and misunderstanding can be caused by hastily expressed zeal on one side, and lack of patience on the other side, sometimes creating entrenched antagonisms

which are not easily afterwards healed. While we need the
toleration and understanding shown by Elijah, we also need
to remember his '*remember*'.

What did the Lord do to *us* and say to *us* when we were
baptised in his name? What does he continually do and say to
us when we come to his holy table and receive from him the
bread and wine? We, too, are meant to remember, and are
reminded by these signs that we belong to him and are no
longer our own.

Points for Further Thought and Discussion

Even though God was with him, Elijah was for a considerable time deprived of the sense of God's presence which he had previously learned to expect. Can you think of other Old Testament. writers or characters to whom this happened? Should we expect our own New Testament experience to be similar to Elijah's?

Reformed theologians distinguished between the 'active obedience' of Jesus (e.g. his vigorous ministry of teaching and miracle in Galilee) and his 'passive obedience' (i.e. the suffering and rejection he bore on his way to the Cross). They affirmed that he accomplishes our redemption through both aspects of his work, and sets an example for us. Do we ourselves in the offering of our lives to God, tend to think that we can please him effectively only through our engagement in Christian activity, forgetting his desire for us to glorify him also through obedient acceptance of whatever suffering he lays on us. Cf.. De Sales advice: 'We must have patience not only to be ill, but to be ill with the illness which God wills, in the place where He wills, and amongst such persons as He wills; and so of other tribulations.'

What features of the call of Elisha are common to the accounts of the calls given by Jesus to his disciples in the Gospel stories? Under what circumstances may we ourselves expect to hear this call today?

God at this time holds on to Israel as his people not only because of the work and leadership of Elijah, but also because there were 7000 who had not 'bowed the knee'. Jesus said of his disciples 'You are the salt of the earth' (the preservative of the community!). Think out the encouragement and the challenge these facts give us today.

Elijah, partially rebuked for taking the sword to slaughter the priests, was nevertheless told by God to depend on others to use the sword he himself was forbidden to take. Has this Word of God something positive to say to us today (cf. Romans 13: 1–4).

Notes

The Angel

When the phrase the 'Angel of the Lord' is used in the Old Testament often it refers to a quite unique 'heavenly being sent by God to deal with men as his personal agent and spokesman.' This person has been referred to as a 'mighty and mysterious being' and sometimes has a prominent place in theophanies (see accompanying note). Sometimes he so closely represents God as to be identified with him. (cf. Gen. 16:7ff.; 22:11ff.; 31:31; Ex. 3:2; Judges 6:11–23 etc.). When associated with the Spirit, it has been held that the Old Testament has a doctrine of the Trinity.

In this present incident, the ministry of 'an Angel of the Lord', however, need indicate simply the service of one of those many created spiritual beings who are messengers and witnesses of the divine will, can providentially under God's direction exercise care for human beings, and help to bring about his judgements (cf. Ps. 78:49; Ps. 91:11f.)

The Theophany

In the Old Testament there are certain (often dramatic) occasions called 'theophanies' when God comes unusually near to those to whom he wills to speak, and there occurs what has been called a 'more direct inbreaking of the divine into the human experience than is normal'. Sometimes in such encounters God gives visible signs (e.g. like fire) of his near presence, or audible signs (e.g. like thunder or as here 'an awesome whisper'). Elijah's experience at the mouth of the cave, or that of Moses at the burning bush (cf. Exod. 19:10–20) deserve to be called 'theophanies'. Less dramatic but no less real a theophany was the appearance of the 'Angel of the Lord' to Gideon or Manoah and his wife (Judges 6:11ff; 13:2–23). It is characteristic that those who experience such happenings recognise the unusual nearness of God, tremble, veil their faces, and are filled with wonder that they have lived through them (Gen. 32:30; Judges 13:22–4). Such experiences differ from mere visions in which often real distance is felt between what is seen and the subject involved.

Elijah's Mantle

Prophets or 'men of God' often wore a distinctive dress by which their profession was recognised. To become a prophet could be referred to in popular speech as 'to put on a hairy mantle' (Zech. 13:4). This was a cloak made of animal hair. John the Baptist wore such a mantle as a sign that he was the successor to Elijah (Matt. 3:4).

CHAPTER XIV

A DOUBLE MINDED MAN
1 Kings 20

The Narrative

Ahab, courageously, and apparently with true religious zeal, resists and overcomes an attack by the king of Aram on Samaria. In doing so he consults the prophets of the Lord, accepts their guidance, and wins their support. In a further attack by the Arameans, the following year, the honour of God's name can be vindicated only by the death of the blasphemous king. They again support Ahab and the war is won. But Ahab in the hour of his triumph shows his instability and his double-mindedness by courting the friendship of God's avowed enemy. He is openly condemned by a leading prophet and becomes alienated and resentful.

(Note: Where the R.S.V. has 'Syria and Syrian', we have preferred to use 'Aram and Aramean.)

Ahab Among the Prophets

It was Jezebel and not Ahab who threatened to kill Elijah after Carmel. Even she, however, no doubt because of the change in public opinion towards Elijah, was unable to pursue her threat. In that political and religious climate all the prophets of the Lord began again to make their influence felt. Ahab himself seemed inclined to turn back to the faith of his fathers, and for a short time his bearing and behaviour remind us that he had the qualities that might have made him a good king – had it not been for Jezebel. The purpose of the next three

142

chapters of the book of Kings is to show how the tension between Ahab and the prophets round Elijah revived and grew; and how, finally, he met his death by ignoring and defying the word they proclaimed.

Our present chapter opens with an invasion of Israel by its enemy in the north, the army of Aram. King Ben-hadad seems already to have defeated Israel in a previous battle. Imperiously demanding his due tribute he has surrounded the city of Samaria. At first Ahab is inclined to agree to his cruel terms. As these become more outrageous and arrogant, however, Ahab reacts. In a series of consultations he puts the case before the elders and the people, and they, too, decide to assist. It is a courageous move. Ben-hadad boasts that he can reduce Samaria to dust and has enough men to carry it all away in handfuls!

The history of Israel can contain no more noble account of the conduct of a believing and courageous king facing overwhelming odds than Ahab's relief of the siege of Samaria. All the ingredients of a great victory for God based on morale and trust are here. Certainly the enemy stupefy themselves with drink. Their intelligence proves inadequate and God, as he often does with Israel's enemies, allows them first to indulge in empty boasting, then to become seized by panic. In the end a complete victory is won by the action of only a selected few from Israel. Ahab, throughout, is disciplined, courageous and rises to great dignity in his inspired proverbial utterance: '*Let not him that girds on his armour boast himself as he that puts it off*' (v. 11). He humbly consults his men of God, and accepts their guidance.

The prophets are proud of their king. They no doubt imagined that Elijah's witness and work on Carmel had made its mark on him, and that they now faced a future for Israel full of promise. It was they who took the initiative in warning him that the defeated enemy would attack again, the following year, so that he could plan for the next battle. Again, before the battle was engaged at Aphek, confident that he would respond with true faith, they brought him a message from the Lord as he faced what seemed another hopeless situation; '*Have you seen all this great multitude? Behold, I will give it into your hand this day; and you will know that I am the Lord*' (v. 13). God did his part well, inspiring the few with insuperable skill and courage, demoralising those against him, and bringing down a city to add to the already enormous devastation *'Ben-hadad fled to the city and hid in an inner room'* (v. 30, N.I.V.).

'Ben-hadad my brother'

It was at this juncture that the shock came for many of the prophets who had been there on the field with Ahab giving their support. They felt betrayed as they watched their king giving favour and honour to the defeated enemy, and discovered how far his thoughts and ways were from their own.

The cause of their dismay and anger lay in the unique nature of the challenge which the Arameans had issued to Israel before this second battle. Their wise men had attacked the claims made by Israel about the unique power and greatness of their God, and they had made the approaching battle into a defiant challenge to his reputation. It was true, they argued, that he had beaten them at Samaria but that defeat was due merely to the fact that he had lured them into his territory. He was indeed a purely local God and his power held good only in the valleys round about his city. Let the Israelites come out to war again – this time in the hills beyond his reach, and it would soon be shown that Israel's claim to his universal sovereignty was mere empty talk! It was calculated blasphemy directed against the name of the Lord. It called in question everything Israel's prophets were preaching. To them it made the coming war a holy war that Israel could not fail to win, and Ahab was now in their eyes like a second David entering battle against a boasting pagan Goliath, defiant of the living God! He was the defender and champion of everything that Israel's faith stood for. They believed it was impossible for him to fail, and of one thing they were certain that the insult to their God could be purged, and his name vindicated, only through complete and decisive victory involving the death of Ben-hadad who had dared to defy so openly the living God. They had made it clear to Ahab that God had put the Aramean king under the ban – an irrevocable decree consigning him to immediate and utter destruction when he was taken. Ben-hadad knew enough about the situation to expect such death, and went into hiding. His officials, however, inspired him with a faint hope of survival, and they made a plot. They would go and show themselves to their victor dressed in sack-cloth and ropes to symbolise their willingness to accept humbly whatever bondage he decreed. Israel's kings had, after all, a reputation of sometimes being generous to enemies.

Ahab amazed at their humility before him, and their pretence of sincerity, was trapped into talking to them as if they were still on his own level.. They knew immediately from his reaction that they were going to succeed. Their abject display had made the triumphant king suddenly feel more important than ever before in his life – an enemy at his feet! He felt a momentary glow of personal greatness and he wanted to display it. How great he would become and how much personal satisfaction it would add to his moment if he could show his magnanimity by giving pardon to his enemy – especially if he now embraced him publicly in his misery! Where was he? '*Is he still alive? He is my brother*!' (v. 33) He had taken their bait! '*Yes*,' they replied '*your brother*'! Ben-hadad received immediate honour, and easy peace terms. Ahab's decision had, however, important personal consequences. It brought about a serious rift between himself and the prophets.

A Final Rift

Some commentators at this point in the story, have regarded Ahab's part in the whole affair as enlightened and progressive. They have accordingly criticised the prophets who opposed him as prejudiced and reactionary. The facts of the case give us no ground for such judgement. The next chapter will show what they already well knew, that Ahab was a man without pity, who had no distaste for murder when it was to his advantage. They therefore felt shock and disgust when they heard of the invitation to Ben-hadad to come into his chariot, and the showy brotherly embrace. Their verdict on him is easy to understand.

He had been given the opportunity to show his devotion and obedience to the Lord by executing his clear and irrevocable command to slay this blasphemer who was under

God's ban. Instead, he had seized the occasion opened before him for a contemptible display of self-importance. It had been beyond his wildest dreams ever to be in a position to sit in judgement over such a powerful earthly king. He had forgotten that his power had been given to him only to obey the clear word that had already come to him from God. He had, further, shown a complete lack of concern over the issues that had been at stake in the battle to vindicate the name of the Lord. Now in their eyes, all the personal bravery and dedication to the Lord that Ahab had seemed to show as he had been with them on the battle field, and his pious support of their cause, appeared to have been merely a clever sham.

He had also shown himself to have had no appreciation of what it had cost his loyal supporters to win victory. They had been brave. Many had lost their lives. Many had been wounded and maimed. In the memory of the prophets there was the story of a leader like David. One day on the battlefield he had been overheard to sigh, expressing a wish that someone would bring him ' a drink of water from the well near the gate of Bethlehem'. The place was in Philistine hands but three of his devoted followers heard him and risked their lives in a fight to bring him the precious water. He refused even to taste it, regarding it as having been bought with the 'blood of men' who had almost sacrificed their lives to win it – and in humble gratitude and appreciation he poured it out 'before the Lord' (2 Sam. 23:13–17). With such a story in their mind it filled them with contempt that this successor of David should have devoted the cup of victory which symbolised so much sacrificial blood, to glorify himself and satisfy his personal vanity. One member of the group of prophets which had so far supported Ahab felt himself impelled by a word from God to express the divine condemnation of his king, and to pronounce the sentence of coming punishment.

The problem before the prophet in seeking to fulfil his unwelcome task was how to get the king seriously to listen to his accusation and admit his error. It was even logistically a difficult task. Ahab on his way back from the battlefield was on a crest of a wave of enormous popularity. He was elated with his success and thrilled with the praise he was receiving for the very behaviour that now had to be condemned. How could he, a solitary prophet, as an individual, break in and gain an audience? How could the king be led even to consider that he might be in the wrong? Again it is possible that the prophet found guidance in the story of David. When the latter was temporarily hardened, strangely, in heart, and had become puffed up with self-importance like Ahab, God's condemnation had been brought home to him by Nathan the prophet. Nathan had simply told a story, had trapped the king into making a judgement condemning the chief actor in the story, and had then turned his judgement back on himself, by pointing the finger at him and saying, 'You are the man' (2 Sam. 12:1–7). Our prophet here made up his own story. He would act it out. He would wait by the roadside as Ahab passed by, and pose as a man who had done exactly what Ahab had done – set free a condemned man with an enormous price on his head. He would elicit Ahab's condemnation, then he would say 'You are the man' and pronounce God's sentence. To make sure that the king would stop, listen, give heed, and realise that he was being confronted with a matter of life and death, the prophet felt he had to have genuine wounds on his body, and blood on his clothes. He believed that this blood was to be a necessary seal to his message which would convince the King that he was speaking in deadly earnest.

It all happened exactly as he planned. Ahab stopped and listened, made exactly the intended judgement on the situation and heard the sentence pronounced upon himself as if it was a word from the living God. He showed his true colours. He did not dare vent the anger he felt upon the messenger who had so cunningly trapped him, but he did not repent. '*The king of Israel went to his house resentful and sullen*' (v. 43).

A remarkable feature of the story, as it is told here, is its revelation of how God in those days worked amongst the divisions and tensions within the prophetic communities (cf. p.88). In this case they were divided in their opinion as to whether or not Ahab should be so bluntly condemned. When it was known what our prophet had been called by God to do, opposition was shown, and one prophet actively refused to co-operate. Great fear must have come over the prophetic community when the prophet who resisted the call of God in

this matter received the sentence of death and was speedily
executed. It was in the eyes of God an infinitely serious matter
to seek to quench the Spirit, or to hinder in any way the
fulfilment of his word, especially when the opposition came
from one who was himself wholly committed to its service.
The case of Ananias and Sapphira proves that the New
Testament in this matter is no less intolerant than the Old
(Acts 5: 1–6).

Points for Further Thought and Discussion

Under the Old Covenant the prophets at times felt justified
not only in giving support to their rulers in their battles,
but also in directing the battle. How far have things changed
for us as Christians and as a Church today? What can be
expected of us and of the Church in the way of support for
a "just war".

A Scottish preacher once published a provocative
sermon on the text of verse 28, pointing out that we, too,
limit God's power to work in our lives by our restricted
idea of the sphere of his Lordship. Think out some of these
ways in which at times we fail by not realising how far his
power really extends.

Ahab's sin was that he de-valued what the men of his army,
under God, had risked their lives to achieve. Does our
tolerance, and easy acceptance of the ways of the world do
justice to the fact that Christ has died to make us hate what he
condemned to destruction on the cross?

The prophet, who here accosted Ahab, cleverly absorbed his
attention in what he thought was as an important story, and
trapped him into making a judgement through which he found
himself accusing himself. Can you think of parables in the teaching
of Jesus where he employs the same approach, i.e., of getting us
to make judgements about given situations and actions, and then
suggesting that we relate them to our own selves?

Can you think of any way in which the danger can be
incurred today of resisting the Holy Spirit (cf. Acts 7:51)

Notes

On 1 Kings chapters 20–22
We now come, in our reading of Kings to a series of stories in
which Ahab is named as the central character. Scholars have no
doubt about the genuineness and importance of the story of

Naboth's vineyard, but they express difficulties in accepting that
some of the other stories originally referred to Ahab. Since the
phrase 'the King of Israel' is so often used of Israel's leader, in
the narrative of chapter 20, some think the two Ahab references
are later insertions, and that the story refers to some king other
than he. The difficulties are caused by an important inscription
which describes the battle of Karkar in which Ahab is mentioned
on the side of a coalition of kings including Ben Hadad fighting
against the Emperor of Assyria. This battle took place in 583.
The problem is: how Ahab fought the three wars against Syria
in three years (cf. 22:1) and appeared also as an ally of Syria at
the battle of Karkar. Some think there is a muddle in dates and
that the three wars mentioned were fought after Karkar. A recent
conservative commentator D. J. Wiseman suggested that the two
wars in chapter 20 were earlier, and that the three years interval
could have allowed a preparation of the final alliance of Israel
and Syria at Karkar in the August of the year in which Ahab
later turned against Syria and died. We believe that the final
editor though he was distant from the events was in a good
position to make sound judgement and was honest in his use of
the material. What concerned him most, however, was to show
how Ahab especially when he was apart from Jezebel was, at first
inclined, after Carmel, to seek the alliance of the Lord and the
support of his true prophets. After a short period he however
found himself alienated from them, then giving himself over to
the influence of his wife he deliberately followed example of
appointing his own prophets. These chapters show how after
Carmel the chief factor determining the fate of Ahab was his
attitude to the Word of God.

The Numbers in Battle
The thirty two 'kings' were 'minor tribal chiefs' who were later
replaced by more experienced commanders.

   Difficulties are naturally felt over the number of casualties
in the war at Aphek (100,000 in one day!) and the statement
that the wall of that city fell on 27,000, the total number left
there. The army of Israel must have been comparatively much
smaller. It is sometimes suggested that it was always traditional
practice in such accounts to exaggerate, that the enumeration
was not meant to be accepted as exact. It has also been pointed

out that the word for a thousand with a very slight possible manuscript emendation could be translated 'officer'.

Ben-hadad -*'devoted to destruction'*

The God of Israel desired the salvation of all mankind, and made his sun 'to rise upon the just and the unjust, and upon the evil and the good.' (Matt. 5:45). Early in the history of Israel, however, he met a vicious form of opposition which had to be crushed if his purpose of love was to be fulfilled. Amalek (cf. Exod. 17:8ff.) without cause or provocation attacked a defenceless and exhausted Israel on their journey in the wilderness, determined to annihilate them in an utterly ruthless way. God had to step in to deliver them by miracle. After the incident God sentenced Amalek to eventual annihilation as a people, and set their form of opposition up as an example for every age to ponder (Exod. 17:14). He declared what became known as a 'Holy War' or a 'ban' against Amalek devoting the whole nation, every individual and all property to total destruction. It was Saul's reaction against what seemed the ruthless nature of this 'ban' that caused God to reject him (cf. 1 Sam. 15). The same 'ban' was extended later to any city in Israel which allowed itself as a whole community to be led treacherously to serve other gods (cf. Deut. 13:12ff.) Undoubtedly in the mind of the prophet who accosted Ahab, the insult which Ben-hadad had uttered against God, his ruthless determination to annihilate Israel, had brought him under this 'ban', and Ahab, he believed, had been made aware of this by God. His conviction about this was so strong that he had himself slashed with a sword in pursuit of his mission.

The 'Sons of the Prophets'

During the days of Samuel we read of 'prophets' in Israel who tended to travel, work, and express their gifts together in groups (1 Sam. 10:9ff.; 19:18ff.) and it is especially during the period dominated by the ministry of Elijah and Elisha that we now often hear of groups called the 'sons of prophets' drawn together here and there. They regarded the two great prophets as their leaders. Though they could marry and have children, they seemed to work and share and learn together, consult each other, and at times differ.

CHAPTER XV

BAAL AND BONDAGE
1 Kings 21

The Narrative

The falsehood of Tyrian Baalism was fully exposed at
Carmel, and its ultimate defeat was ensured. Yet it had by
then obtained a deep foothold on Israel's life, and it was
only during the next generation that it was finally
destroyed. This chapter illustrates the devastating
consequences of the influence of Jezebel and her religion
on both the community life of Israel and on the personal
life of Ahab. Yet it reminds us that God is there in the
midst, watching, waiting and ensuring that in the long
run justice will prevail.

Jezebel Takes Over

Ahab had ambitious plans to enlarge his palace in Samaria. To
fulfil them he had to acquire the family vineyard of Naboth
the Jezreelite which he wanted to incorporate within the
grounds as a herb garden. He visited Naboth with a plan to
purchase the land from him offering beneficial terms. If
Naboth did not want money he could give him a larger place
in a better situation. The transaction he was proposing was in
his eyes allowable by law, and was in accordance with accepted
practice in Israel. His terms were exceedingly generous and it
did not occur to him that Naboth would be foolish enough to
refuse.

That such a proposition could be made– and by his king!–
however, shocked Naboth. To him one of the most sacred laws

of the Lord, was that no man could ever sell his land. 'The land shall not be sold in perpetuity , for the land is mine' (Lev. 25:23). Land was considered as given by God to the people. It was regarded as a threat to the brotherhood, peace, and family life in the community for a man to sell his land, or for another, even the king, to offer to purchase it. To Naboth the religious and legal tradition in Israel did not allow for anyone, even the king, to acquire great estates. He could remember Samuel's warnings against the greed of royal power (1 Sam. 8:14) and the traditional teaching of his faith on the limitations of kingship (Deut. 17:14–20). He turned on Ahab with enraged contempt and dismissed him from his house. The king was bribing him to sin. *'The Lord forbid that I should give you the inheritance of my fathers.'*

The rebuke went home. Ahab knew that he had been a fool even to think of making such an approach to such a man, and his conscience troubled him. Mortified and humiliated, yet also *'vexed and sullen'*, he lay on his bed and turned his face to the wall when people spoke to him or offered him food.

When Jezebel heard his complaint, she tormented him: Was he a king or a puppet in his realm? She would take over this affair and he could relax. 'Cheer up,' she said to him. He could forget about conscience, the Lord and his Law. She would show him how a king should govern a kingdom. She would get him what he wanted.

It was easily and skilfully accomplished. She had her band of special agents trained to work for her. She had the local authorities under her power by now. Some of them were no doubt waiting to receive the contract for building the extensions to the palace. Though she despised the law of the Lord, she now used it. The Law stated (see Lev. 24:16; Deut. 17:16; 19:15) that if it could be proved on the evidence of two witnesses that anyone was guilty of blasphemy, he was to be stoned to death. To curse the king was also a capital offence (Exod. 22:28). She wrote the letters, executed the plot and within a few weeks Naboth was dead. Ahab himself was not actively involved until she came to him with the news: 'Get up and take possession of the vineyard... for Naboth is not alive, but dead' (v.15). This story stands here primarily as an illustration of the subtle and radical change that came over the community life of the people of God when they lost touch with the living God, their sense of his reality, and allowed Baal religion to influence their thought and behaviour. A prominent Old Testament scholar of his day, Wilhelm Vischer, in illustration of what happened here, refers to a dominant characteristic of the natural world around us – that strength prevails over weakness. In the garden is it not the great and well rooted that have more right to survive and grow than the weak? And in the animal world is there not a rule that the strong prey on the defenceless? He pursues the thought that Jezebel , in the way that she behaved here, was simply, whether consciously or unconsciously, acting out her Baalism unrestrainedly. 'The cult of nature worship' he affirms 'is always the dance round the Golden Calf'. Baal religion might seem to seduce by what is wildly beautiful, but at the same time it opened its devotees to what is wildly cruel and self-centred.

A well known verse from the Book of Proverbs is applicable to the situation now in Israel. 'Where there is no revelation, the people cast off restraint' (Prov. 28:19 N.I.V.). The introduction of tyranny or dictatorship within a community is often accompanied by the introduction of doctrines supporting it, and too often people have been robbed of a tradition that safeguarded liberty by allowing their religious thought and practice to become more and more corrupted by falsehood.

What happened in Israel reminds us of the great affirmation of the apostle Paul about liberty: 'Where the Spirit of the Lord is, there is freedom' (2 Cor. 3:17). We make a mistake when we imagine that political liberty is something that is won and kept only by political and economic forces and methods. The true political liberty which can bring security and satisfaction to the free individual in the midst of a free community is the gift of the Spirit of God, and it can be fostered and kept within a nation only as men allow the true and living God who has revealed himself in Jesus Christ to be proclaimed and worshipped without hindrance or neglect.

The Man Who Sold Himself

Though its political implications no doubt reflect the primary importance of this story, we must recognise that it is told here within a series specially devoted to the career of Ahab, and we are meant to study also what it tells us about this king. We have already noted how unreliable he became at the prime of his life. Yet there are indications that there once was a genuinely good side of this man. Old Testament scholars and commentators who try to give a balanced judgement on what can be discovered about him from the Bible and contemporary inscriptions, sometimes praise him as being a good and brave ruler unappreciated by the narrow minded prophets around him. Certainly he seems in his earlier days to have had some potential for the service of the Lord. It has been pointed out that all his children when they were born were given names devoting them to the God of Israel – even the daughter who later became as murderous and abandoned as her mother was called Athaliah! In this present incident we must note that he became immediately ashamed rather than angry in reaction to Naboth's righteous rebuke – no doubt because he had still the stirrings of a bad conscience.

It is against this background of his potential goodness that we are meant to allow a deeply tragic aspect of this story told in this chapter to come home to us. It shows us the havoc worked by evil not only in the nation of Israel, but also in the personal life of Ahab, through his allowing the influence of Jezebel, her culture and her religion to dominate him. It shows the harvest of bitterness and sorrow that he reaped, and the depth of degradation and shame into which he was plunged, almost against his own will and judgement, through the decision he made when he married her and put himself under her power. Ahab is spoken of in this chapter as a man who, joining Jezebel in sin, '*sold himself to do what was evil in the sight of the Lord*' (v.25) and in an earlier chapter it is clearly stated that his marriage with Jezebel was the one sin which displeased God more than anything else he did in his life. It was through this marriage that 'he sold himself' to work whatever evil was the will of his wife (cf. 16:30–33).

When he married he thought he could compromise. He wanted to retain at least a decent measure of alliance with what was best in the laws and traditions of Israel. He also wanted what the alliance with Jezebel seemed to offer. The story shows how hopelessly he floundered. It is said that the English king, William Rufus, had a picture of God on one side of his shield and a picture of the devil on the other with the motto underneath, 'Ready for either'. Ahab gives us a truer picture of the man who compromises. He was ready for neither. He had no answer for Naboth. He could not stand before his face. But neither could he withstand Jezebel. When she entered the room and found him sulking she taunted him about his weakness and stupidity. He had to yield himself now, submissive, into her hands. He was beaten and she could do what she liked.

We can recognise the tragic situation of Ahab in many life situations around us today. One evil person can so dominate and influence others of weaker character that they descend to depths of evil to which by themselves they could never have sunk. A gang or a group can make criminals or addicts out of individuals who, left to themselves, would go straight (cf. Exod. 23:2).

We can also recognise Jezebel. She was pitiless, abandoned to evil, beyond conscience or the possibility of repentance, with an especially intense hatred of the order and purposes which Israel's tradition stood for. Are we not discovering that there are many around us today, who having been given the liberty to show the depravity of mind and heart from which Christ has come to deliver us, are freely displaying their likeness to her – bent on destroying justice, raping and abusing purity and goodness and on bringing everything and everyone around them down to their own level? The New Testament teaching about the nature and origin of sin and evil suggests that we should see behind Jezebel's ruthless nihilistic determination to obliterate all goodness and truth around her, a sign that there is at work in the sphere of human life powers of evil, of a personal nature, which we often call 'satanic'. They are continually at work around us in society seeking to destroy God's loving purposes in human life. They seek the alliance of others in their purpose to thwart and pervert the work of God. Their origin is a mystery. Jesus affirmed that Satan was ' a murderer from the beginning' (John 8:44) But his work among us is tragically real and 'devilish'. No woman by herself could have made herself Jezebel. New Testament teaching also suggests that within the personal plight of a man like Ahab we should see evidence not simply of the work of evil on a human level but of the activity of this same evil power seeking to extend its kingdom. Jesus once warned even the apostle Peter that he was in danger of falling under bondage more tragic than that which enslaved Ahab. He could only be saved from it by Jesus' prayers. 'Simon, Simon, Satan has asked to sift you as wheat. But I have prayed for you' (Luke 22:31).

After Carmel Jezebel had still power, but it was a phantom power, the power of a defeated enemy seeking, on retreat, to do damage, in the short time before the inevitable final sentence on her was executed (Rev. 12:12). After Calvary, the defeated powers of evil on their way to final destruction are still around us. This is why the New Testament gives us so many warnings to watch and pray (Matt. 26:41; I Cor. 16:13; I Thess. 5:6) against our adversary the devil (I Pet. 5:8).

Yet how few these warnings are, compared with the continually echoed call to rejoice in the glorious liberty of the children of God!

The Watching and Waiting God

We may ask: Why did God not protect and vindicate this good man Naboth immediately? Murder, perjury and theft have taken place and he has seemed to do nothing.

Christ alone gives us the true and final answer to such a question. The story, however, gives an answer which assured people in those days that it was worth holding on to their faith and fighting for it. God, they are told, is watching and waiting.

As Ahab stood an the middle of the vineyard, surveying the property, planning the lay-out of his new garden, a voice arrested him: '*Have you not murdered a man and seized his property?*' (v.19 N.I.V.). Elijah had been sent by God to confront him. Though God did not save Naboth, he sought out his murderer with unerring justice. Every hidden detail of the event, the thoughts of those involved, their secret conversations, and their plans are all seen and known by him and are recorded in his book, to be revealed and judged when he decides the time. This encounter between Elijah and Ahab in the vineyard is a sign that a final judgement will take place.

Elijah placed full responsibility on Ahab's shoulders for what happened. Ahab may even be tempted to tell himself that it was not he, but Jezebel, who had done the act. In the eyes of God, however, we are guilty of the sins we are involved in through our weakness and carelessness as if we had actively planned them. '*So you have found me, my enemy?*' (v.20), Ahab cried out in dismay when he found himself confronted by the dreaded presence of Elijah. God is the One who finds men. He finds men in the depths of their iniquity. He finds men in order either to free them and forgive them, or to judge them. Who knows, whether even at that late hour, Elijah might have been sent to save Ahab if, instead of calling God his enemy, he had decided from then on to call God his friend! He almost did so. As we read on we are given an astonishing account of how he plunged into a mood of deep remorse and put on sackcloth, a sign of mourning. God decided to delay the judgement which had been pronounced on him by Elijah. Time was given him to prove whether there was sincerity in his heart.

We are to discover at the beginning of the next chapter that God's amazing patience and hope were in vain. The Ahab we meet there has finally decided that his decision before Elijah was made in a weak moment of irrational fear and weakness. Jezebel is still there from day to day to work her will. The roots of the good seed which had begun to shoot out so promisingly, strike the rock and wither (Matt. 13:20–21).

Points for Further Thought and Discussion

Ahab (like Esau cf. Gen. 25:34) had lost respect for the tradition that Naboth regarded as safeguarding '*the heritage of my fathers*'. Are we in danger of going the same way, to our own tragic loss? Think of ways and directions that this might be happening.

The story as we have it from the writer, does not introduce the concept of Satanic power in the way we have it in the New Testament. Are we justified here in suggesting that evil powers, explainable only as entering our life from beyond the range of what is purely human, have entered human affairs, taken control, and worked havoc in the human situation – and that the same can happen today, apart from God's grace and power? Can you think of definite instances? Is this the reason why Christ warned us so much to 'watch'?

Ahab would never have done it himself, but he knew what was happening and did nothing to stop it. How guilty was he? Are we challenged here to expose public wrong-doing by those in authority – as an urgent duty? Is our modern media exposure of public scandal in high places a healthy factor in modern society?

Be sure your sin will find you out! (Num. 32:23) Read about the vision of final judgement in Rev. 20:11 – 15). Can life, and the teaching of Jesus possibly have meaning unless what this signifies actually does take place? Should we hear much more about this from the Church?

Notes

Aspects of the Land Law in Israel
The land was originally distributed among the people of Israel by a lot which was regarded as under the supervision of God himself (Nu. 26:55). It had always to be regarded by its possessors as a loan from God That it did not belong to themselves was emphasised by the custom of the Sabbatical year in which all loans were cancelled (Deut. 15:2) and the land was not sown by its 'owner' but was set aside as a gift from

God himself, the true owner (Lev. 25:4–5; Exod. 23:10). It was at the year of Jubilee (every 50th year) that all alienated property was restored to its rightful owner (Lev. 25:13). It is possible that through such land arrangements Israel was being taught to look forward to the age of the coming Messiah.

It is worth-while, in estimating the attitude of Naboth, to consider that he may have regarded Omri, the father of Ahab as being of Canaanite origin, and therefore his son had no right to own land in Israel.

Jezebel's plot

D.J. Wiseman in his recent commentary reminds us at this point that it was a custom in any national emergency to proclaim a day of fasting. A contemporary famine may have been the cause for such an announcement. On such an occasion if the person who caused the disaster could be identified he would be sentenced to stoning (cf. 1 Sam. 14:40–45; Josh. 7:16–26). Jezebel called for the occasion, arranged for Naboth to be seated prominently before the people, and for two witnesses to swear that it was he who had committed the crime which had brought about the disaster. The false witnesses recalled in a garbled form what he had said when he refused to sell his land to the king, implying that he had cursed God and the king (cf. Deut. 17:6–7; Exod. 22:28) and demanded the death sentence. She was thorough. We later learn that she contrived to have Naboth's sons put to death with their father (cf. 2 Kings 9:26). This would exclude any possibility of their claiming the inheritance. The king in any case had royal rights to the property of a criminal.

The Jezebel-Ahab relationship

It should be noted by the reader that we have given an interpretation of the Jezebel -Ahab relationship in the light cast on it by the New Testament teaching rather than that explicit in the Old Testament. 'Satan' was then pictured as an angelic servant of God subject to him and at times engaged in activities that could be harmful (1 Chron 21:1; Zech. 3:1ff.), but is not seen as having the overwhelming malignance and power accorded to him in the New Testament. It was during the development of Judaistic thought in the period between the Testaments, that the idea of demonic powers threatening mankind's destiny came to light. It was Christ in his life and death who revealed the reality and intensity of the evil power he had come to destroy, and the crucial nature of the struggle. It was Paul who developed the conception of men and women personally under the bondage of Satan, which we have used in the interpretation of our text. We believe that this application of New Testament teaching to the interpretation of the Old is justifiable.

CHAPTER XVI

THE AFFAIR OF RAMOTH GILEAD
I Kings 22

The Narrative

Ahab, planning a military campaign to recapture
Ramoth Gilead from the Arameans seeks the alliance
of Jehoshaphat, king of Judah, who is making a friendly
visit to Samaria. Knowing Jehoshaphat's religious
concern he has arranged support for his expedition
from a group of official royal prophets under his
control. He still finds Jehoshaphat reluctant till he
hears a word from a better attested 'prophet of the
Lord'. Micaiah is therefore summoned to give his
opinion, while Ahab and his 'prophets' continue to use
every means at their disposal to intensify the already
mounting enthusiasm for the venture, so that even
Jehoshaphat becomes convinced. Micaiah is punished
for his opposing opinion, and his warnings fall on deaf
ears. Ahab goes to his death, and Jehoshaphat narrowly
escapes disaster.

The Human Situation

Before Ahab summoned Micaiah into his presence to give his
opinion about his proposed expedition to Ramoth Gilead, he
had seen to it that the lonely prophet would not be listened to
if he disapproved. Micaiah had been brought into the situation
only by a quite unlooked for request from King Jehoshaphat
to hear an extra opinion from a well established '*prophet of the
Lord*' (v. 7).

The situation arose, in the first place, because Ahab had been seized by an overwhelming desire to go and recapture Ramoth. It was a border town, traditionally belonging to Israel which had fallen into the possession of his neighbour the king of Aram. Though he had been promised its return when he defeated Ben-hadad (see p.145) it had not yet been given up. He was especially concerned to have it, because it could give him protection on his southern flank in view of dangers which he saw arising within the developing international situation. He believed that if he could obtain the alliance of Jehoshaphat the king of Judah he could take it.

He seized his opportunity when the latter visited him. No doubt it was after a display of his troops, and a review of his chariots and horsemen, that he found his visitor favourably inclined. It is a remarkable feature of this visit of Jehoshaphat that Ahab was also prepared to impress and encourage his visitor with a strong religious backing. Ahab by this time, as we have (cf. pp.145ff) had fallen out with the independent prophets of the Lord whose ways and opinions he resented. He had appointed and trained an impressive group of his own royal prophets to back up his enterprise after the pattern of his wife's Baal prophets. He had known that Jehoshaphat, a king who had a reputation for the fear of God, would never risk a war without consulting his men of God. What he had not quite bargained for, however, was that Jehoshaphat should suspect the integrity of such a large and impressively uniformed band of religious men, and make the request, '*Is there not here another prophet of the Lord of whom we can enquire?*' (v.7). It was only then that he had to mention Micaiah and send for him to come. It was a threatening hitch in his planned programme but he was confident that he still had the ability, no matter what Micaiah said, to win through to success.

He had already stage-managed everything flawlessly for the great royal reception at which he hoped to impress the visiting king and his court as he proposed his war alliance. A commodious site with fine vistas at the entrance to his capital had been chosen. He had raised two thrones side by side to match the splendid royal robes that were worn on these occasions. We cannot help admiring the skill with which he controlled the gradually mounting pace of the celebration, raising songs and slogans emphasising now the positive certainty of success, now the Lord's inevitable support, whipping up such enthusiasm that even to imagine dissent was impossible. His prophet Zedekiah gave a demonstration with the use of iron horns of how the Arameans would be gored to destruction, stirring up the belief that his demonstration would have a magical effect on the outcome of the final battle, and the four hundred prophets, all experts in raising the temperature of an occasion by dervish dancing set about their act and claimed victoryin repeating the chorus *'Go up to Ramoth Gilead and triumph, for the Lord will give it into the hand of the king'* (v.12). Ahab, watching and listening, became more and more thrilled and self-confident. Everyone had become so worked up that Micaiah had become irrelevant before he arrived. Ahab had so convinced himself by his own planned display that he had lost all fear of opposition, and was bold enough to dare Micaiah to be a spoil sport if he would. He who seduces others is himself seduced!

The writer, in describing the scene so vividly, is putting across an important message: how delusive a whipped up enthusiasm for anything can become, if it is artfully managed! Bring in the expert in advertising and public relations. Invent the slogans and the songs. Repeat, repeat and repeat. The real quality and worth of what is being offered matters less and less. Moreover, if the issues at stake are serious, religious, or political, people can become immersed in error, a prey to the charlatan, and oriented to self-destruction, and as with Micaiah, dissent and protest will too often find themselves dealt with by brute force.

Micaiah   (1) Prophetic Hesitation

We are meant to notice how hesitant Micaiah was when he was thrust into the midst of this enthusiasm and challenged by Ahab to speak his word from the Lord. At first when he was pressed for his decision he appeared simply to join in the general chorus of assent to what Ahab wanted: *'Go up and triumph'* (v.15). But he spoke in a way that was not meant to be taken seriously. There may have been a note of hesitancy that betrayed the fact that he was merely echoing something of which he was not sure, or perhaps there was a touch of sarcasm in the tone of his voice. Ahab immediately recognised the lack of prophetic conviction, and was impatient.

Micaiah obviously required time to become more fully aware of the situation and attitude of his hearers, and to wait for a word which he knew for certain to have come from God himself, and which he could speak with clarity and full assurance. Of course he had to pray. Possibly he felt he had to prepare his mind and heart to become receptive and submissive to God. Possibly it took time for him to detach himself from the pressure on him simply to say what everybody wanted to hear. Possibly he had to tackle his own natural fear of facing a task that might be extremely difficult (cf. I Sam. 3:15, 17). It was customary for a prophet, suddenly challenged to speak a word from God, to have to wait some time till it came clearly (cf. Jer. 28:6,12).

His hesitancy stands so much in contrast to the superficial way in which we ourselves sometimes interpret the Bible today that it is worth while at this point asking ourselves important questions. Too may of us think that the interpretation of the Word is mainly a matter of using our brains and imagination as well as we can, of consulting our commentaries, of unlocking the text or incident with our well-cut theological key – and we can become so expert by practice that we almost know the answer the moment we read the text. Finding and speaking the Word of God to their contemporaries, however, involved the prophets in a serious struggle to bring every motion of mind and heart into subjection to God in fear and trembling, and in anxiety not to contaminate what the word was saying with their own prejudices and opinions (cf. Dan. 10:10–12). Strangely at this very point it was Ahab who helped Micaiah to prepare himself for the revelation that was soon to come by an unconsciously pointed reminder of what his task was: *'How many times must I make you swear to tell me nothing but the truth, in the name of the Lord'* (v.16, N.I.V.).

Micaiah   (2) Prophetic Certainty

The Word he sought came in the form of two visions, one after the other, each carrying its explanation in spoken words. The first, of all Israel scattered on the hills like sheep without a shepherd, carried the implication that the disastrous loss of the leader would follow the expedition to Ramoth. The second, implied that the Lord himself had put a lying spirit in the mouths of false prophets around Ahab to entice him to court a disaster which God had himself decreed. Micaiah spoke out boldly. It had been his vow as a prophet: '*What the Lord says to me, that I will speak*' (v.14), and he was faithful to it. Moreover Ahab's dramatic challenge to him to speak up honestly, had created a silence in which he was intently heard.

We can imagine the thrill he felt as he spoke so compellingly. He was a prophet of the status of Elijah himself, now standing before the whole nation as Elijah had done at Carmel, and repeating an equally clear Word of God with an equally decisive challenge. Here again, he must have felt, God was going to use him and the prophetic warning he had given, to save the same people from a threatening tragic disaster.

There can be little doubt therefore that he felt disappointed and humiliated by the immediate reaction to his words. Possibly he had expected the personal attack – the slap in the face by the prophet against whom his word had to be so personally aimed. He may also have already steeled himself against the personal anger of the king, even against his possible imprisonment. But all the people were dumb! God had sent no fire from heaven as he had for Elijah, to turn their hearts! Moreover, even godly Jehoshaphat had heard him out, had found him unconvincing, and was throwing his lot on the side of Ahab. Micaiah is here the forerunner of so many of us who are at times given evidence beyond doubt that God is speaking clearly and cogently – and there is no seeming response!

It is in the light of these feelings that we are meant to appreciate and interpret his compelling dramatic last message, just before he was led away to his prison and possible martyrdom: '*Mark my words all you people!*' (v.28 N.I.V.) He had no present visible proof that he had indeed spoken the Word of God – no immediate response, no miraculous sign. Yet he had within him the certainty that God had spoken, and that as he had spoken, Israel had experienced a moment of truth. His word of prophecy which had been given to him to save Israel from going the very way they had now chosen, would therefore now fulfil itself as a word of judgement and doom. History would prove the wisdom, validity and truth of his words, and God would vindicate them by bringing to pass what they decreed.

In the conflict he entered with the ruling powers of his day and in the suffering he experienced at their hands Micaiah reminds us both of Elijah and the nameless prophet who was sent from Judah to Jeroboam. They were all forerunners of the later prophets who have left us their words to read for ourselves in the great prophetic books of the Bible. The similarities are striking. These successors of Micaiah, from Amos to Ezekiel, were all, as he was, dependent upon the word which was given to them from above. Sometimes, like Micaiah here, they received this word by seeing visions and hearing explanations of them. The word had to be waited for, and yielded to with costly effort and submission. They too had often the same perplexing disappointment that their preaching had been in vain and they too suffered persecution. But they had the same certainty as Micaiah that ultimately the word that went forth from their mouth would accomplish what God sent it to do (Isa. 55:11).

The writer to the Hebrews, describing the faith and sufferings of the 'great cloud of witnesses' in the Old Testament with whom we are surrounded as we look to Jesus, was perhaps thinking of Micaiah when he wrote that 'some faced jeers and floggings, while still others were chained and put in prison' (Heb. 11:36) They all looked to Christ, and consciously or unconsciously bore witness to him as they fulfilled their ministry. Moreover, Jesus himself, as he read about them, found much of the pattern of his own ministry in theirs. Of course there were great differences. Jesus' sufferings were beyond anything any prophet could ever have faced. He himself had the word and wisdom of God always there in his possession. He had merely to make his mind known and God had spoken. Yet the one thing they shared with him was their confidence in the word that was spoken.

'Heaven and earth will pass away, but my words will not pass
away' (Matt. 24:31).

Ahab's Death   (1) The Road to Self-destruction

There is a brief passage in the seventh chapter of Paul's Epistle
to the Romans which we can enlist for our attempt to
understand Ahab's mental and emotional make-up as he now
pursues his campaign against Ramoth.

Speaking from his own experience Paul claims that as long
as God did not press him too closely or persistently with his
demands for obedience to his law, he found life tolerable and
could enjoy his self-rule (Rom. 7:9). He was 'alive apart from
the law' But when God really began pressing him for his love
and obedience, with legal demands, he found within himself
a deep and hitherto dormant inner hatred of God's rule, and
indeed, of everything God stood for. The sin that dwelt within
him sprang into action, and showed itself up by producing all
kinds of evil impulses and desires (Rom. 7: 8–10).

At this stage of his life, so hardened had Ahab become
against God and his laws, that instead of deterring him, his
word provoked defiance. It now added a new dimension to his
purpose in going to Ramoth Gilead. He was no longer out
merely to teach the King of Aram a lesson and to win the city,
he was out also, and primarily, to teach the prophets of God a
lesson, and to express the scorn he was now feeling for them.
All his life he has been frustrated by their word. His kingdom
has been troubled, even threatened, by their preaching (cf.
18:17; 20:43; 21:20). Now he has his opportunity to end their
rule of superstition. His expedition will be victorious and when
he returns he will expose the sham. He had sinister thoughts
of the pleasure he would have in settling his account with
Micaiah when he returned. Augustine, thinking back on the
days of his youth asked himself what had possessed him when
one day he had broken into an orchard and stolen some pears?
Why had he wanted and loved those pears? He had not been
hungry and they were not even eaten. Rather, he simply had
found pleasure in doing what God forbade, and he had been
provoked by the 'Thou shalt not'

That 'Ahab disguised himself' (v.29) is significant. Some commentators suggest that this disguise was a fairly common custom followed by some kings in a superstitious attempt to evade the spells that could be cast on them by the magicians of the enemy. It is more likely that the very word he was defying made Ahab uneasy in his defiance of it. He knew the right way and yet he was going the wrong way! His disguise was a sign that he was trying to hide himself from God as well as from the enemy. We can never be care-free or entirely open in pursuing any way of life against which we have heard the Word of God coming to us in one of its many forms. Even in this 'post-Christian era' among those around us who profess to have become 'liberated' from the restraints of their former moral standards, there often remains enough knowledge of Christ, his way of life and the meaning of the Cross, to create a troubled conscience. Jesus affirmed that his Cross, where and when it was lifted up, would disturb and 'cast out' the dominating power of evil from the human heart and at the same time would 'draw all men' to himself (John 12:32) When he said 'all men', he did not mean only those who positively responded to him with faith, but also those who rejected, and chose their own way. They would never be able to free themselves from his disturbing and compelling influence.

Ahab's Death   (2) Accident or Incident?

The sheer inevitability of his death is the fact most heavily underlined in the account of the battle. Things began to go Ahab's way. His disguise worked. The king of Aram had been determined to kill him and had given special instructions to thirty two chariot commanders not to fight with any one but the king of Israel (v. 31). But they diverted their energies and resources in a concentrated attack on the king of Judah. It was only when the latter found himself in extreme peril and *'cried out'* that they recognised the error and called off the plan altogether, Ahab possibly saw this happening and indulged in self congratulations. But *'Someone drew a bow at random and hit the King of Israel between the sections of his armour'* (v.34 N.I.V.), possibly between the chain mail and the breastplate.

Here we are certainly meant to pause and think. Life and history are full of what seems tragically random, like this wildly aimed arrow – senseless, leaderless, uncontrolled, sometimes trivial, sometimes horrific. Yet God was there in the midst of much that seemed futile and accidental on this battlefield, working out his redeeming purpose for mankind in the midst of earth's chaotic and turbulent history and doing so in a hidden, precise and quite marvellous way!

The quiet providentially guided miracle of this obscure archer's arrow can be a sign to us of the hidden way God is wonderfully intervening in the midst of our affairs today. H R MacIntosh, my theology professor, anxious to clear our minds of their prejudice against miracles began his lectures on the subject by asking, 'Do you believe that God can put a thought in a human mind?' 'If so,' he continued, 'then you believe in the miraculous.' A perceptive commentator on this account of the death of Ahab wrote, 'Everyone who does not regard such incidents as accidents must note and understand' We are led on to the final thought that in Jesus God himself has come into the midst of such circumstances to share in our experience of these 'slings and arrows of outrageous fortune' and to overcome the evil powers that have brought such chaos and bondage into our lives, through his life, death and resurrection.

Ahab's Death   (3) Nobility in Shame

We are meant to appreciate the bravery shown by the dying king in the vain attempt to save his army from total defeat. He knew he was mortally wounded and at first pled to be taken out of the fighting. But, realising that the day would be lost if his army knew what had really happened, he had himself propped up in his chariot as if nothing was wrong while his blood drained out on to its floor. It was only as the sun was setting that he finally collapsed, and with this blow the battle was lost. Again, at the hour of his death, we are allowed a glimpse of what some commentators have praised as a truly noble trait of character in this king of Israel. His admirers make the suggestion that the arrow found its entrance only because he was lifting up his arm to rally his troops.

Where Holy Scripture in its world of story shows us things worth admiring we are meant to admire, giving honour to whom honour is due (Rom. 13:7). Saul, like Ahab, died on the battlefield fighting Israel's enemies. He too was rejected by God because of his folly. He too turned against God and his prophets. He seems to have lived a life controlled by jealousy and bitterness, lost all his ideals and met his end as if he were utterly doomed by God. And yet David, lamenting when he heard of his death, remembered the greatness that once was glimpsed in his character and thought, not of the wickedness that had been punished, but only of the tragedy it was that such a great man should come to such a pathetic end: 'Saul and Jonathan, beloved and lovely! In life and death they were not divided.... How are the mighty fallen in the midst of the battle!' (2 Sam. 1:23–25) It sometimes happens that the accounts we are given in Holy Scripture of the death of the wicked are written in such a way as to light up the sheer tragedy and waste they present before the eyes of a God who would have willed otherwise for one who was dear to him.

Jehoshaphat

The main purpose of our writer at this point in the history is to continue to hold our interest within the history of Israel as the conflict with Baalism continues after the death of Ahab and moves towards the climax in the massacre of the whole house of Omri under Jehu. To keep us up to date, however, with what was happening in Judah he inserts brief sections on the affairs of the Southern kingdom. We will thus be well enough informed when we finally come to the account of the ultimate destruction of the influence Jezebel imported even into Judah through her daughter Athaliah.

The description we are given here of Jehoshaphat's kingship in Judah is highly favourable, and in the mention of his refusal to join Ahaziah the son of Ahab in another hazardous enterprise (v. 48), there is an indication that he learned his lesson never again to become involved in dangerous liaisons.

The much more detailed account of Jehosaphat's reign is given by a later writer in 2 Chronicles, occupying four full chapters of the book. It gives us some extra information relevant to our present incident. We are told that Jehoshaphat's cry, when he found himself surrounded by the enemy chariots was a prayer for help which God himself answered, and that when he retired from the battle, a prophet severely condemned him and a punishment followed: 'Should you help the wicked and love those who hate the Lord? Because of this wrath has gone out against you from the Lord'. (2 Chron. 19:2; cf.. 2 Cor. 6:14–15).

Points for Further Thought and Discussion

Can you think of occasions today when we are carried away by contemporary enthusiasms – either to be revolutionary, or to re-establish conventional values, or what, to such an extent that we lose touch with reality and fail to be receptive to the Word of God?

Micaiah was certain of the exact answer he received from God to speak to his hearers. Can we ourselves in the Church be certain and exact in the word we receive from Holy Scripture on any of the problems which face us in our lives? If so give examples of matters on which we can, and matters in which we cannot have certainty.

Is it inevitable today, as it was in the case of Micaiah that witness to the truth , borne by an individual or the Church, should be rejected? At what points, are we, or should we be, suffering such rejection in the world of today?

"If it's got your name on it, you will get it." Think of the cynicism or resignation with which this was often said when the bombs were falling during the second world war, and compare it with the faith with which this writer means us to interpret his account of Ahab's death.

Read 2 Chronicles 19: 1–2, where Jehoshaphat is severely rebuked for his alliance with Ahab, and also 2 Corinthians 6: 14–18. Can you draw lessons for yourself and for the Church?

Notes

God's use of evil
Many commentators seek to be apologetic over the idea that God could really fill the minds of a group of people with a falsehood in order to lead two deluded kings into course threatening self-destruction. But the writer of the story has obviously no qualms about it. Neither had Micaiah (cf. 1 Sam.

16:14; Isa. 19:14; Ps. 18:26–27). The New Testament itself teaches that God not only curbs and controls the activity of evil powers and persons in this world but also uses them to promote his purpose and directs them as he wills even to the extent of creating delusion in their minds (cf. 2 Thess 2:11; Rom 1:24; 9:17–18). It tells the story of how Jesus provoked, controlled, and used the evil reaction of men in working out our salvation on the cross (1 Cor. 2:7–8; Acts 2:23–24).

False Prophets and Prophecy

Jesus teaching in the parable of the 'Tares and the Wheat' illustrates what happens in the important development of prophecy in Israel, in 1 and 2 Kings. In opposition to the word of truth, 'an enemy' seems to be active in promoting falsehood. Tares are sown exactly where good seed is being sown (Matt. 13:24–29,36–42). Jeroboam sets up his false cult in opposition to that of Jerusalem and appoints priests who are not genuine (1 Kings 12:27–30; 13:33–34). Ahab as in this chapter follows him with false prophets and during the history of the monarchy, as true prophecy becomes a more and more influential factor in the nation's life, false prophets and prophecy increase, initiate, confuse and oppose. Jeremiah and Ezekiel especially, speaking out of sad experience have to utter many warnings against the threat of this falsehood (cf. especially Ezek. 13:2ff.; 14:7–11; Jer 14:14; 23:9–22).